EDUCATING PHARAOH

TEENA MYERS

EDUCATING PHARAOH

Published by SCW Publishing

249 Jeffer Dr.

Westwego, LA 70094

ISBN
Paperback 979-8-9873337-3-0
eBook 979-8-9873337-4-7

Cover design and text design by Self Publish Easily
www.selfpublisheasily.com | help@selfpublisheasily.com

Printed in the United States of America

TABLE OF CONTENTS

PREFACE

To follow my thoughts in Educating Pharaoh, you need to understand my concept of faith. I wrote *Faith's Mystery* (2023) as an exposition of Abraham's faith—which is the only faith that pleases God. My writing is built on the foundation of Abraham's faith. You will find *Educating Pharaoh* easier to understand if you read *Faith's Mystery* first.

Educating Pharaoh is part of a longer series of lessons I taught about deliverance based on the exodus of Israel from Egypt. The section about the ten plagues intrigued me. God's aim wasn't to destroy Pharaoh—it was to redeem him so everyone throughout time could know God.

One word drives the story—know. Pharaoh refused to let Israel worship their ancestors' God, because he did not know their God. God wanted Pharaoh to know him. With each plague, Pharaoh grew in the knowledge of who God is, and so does the reader.

God told Pharaoh what he was about to do and his reason for doing it. By the time we reach the tenth plague, Pharaoh knew God. He is calling God Lord, asking Moses to pray for him, admitting he is a sinner and desiring God to bless him. God wanted to bless him, but Pharaoh's pride was in the way.

The problems we wrestle with usually come from authorities who do not know God or who think they are smarter than God. We make our problems worse when we don't know God and embrace lies about him as truth.

The conflicting opinions about God make it difficult to find the truth about him. The Christianity I encountered as a teenager taught that God's deliverance is an individual experience. God delivers individuals. He delivered me from addiction. But pursuing God to solve our problems is a self-centered approach. Jesus said, "But seek first his kingdom and his righteousness, and all these things will be given to you as well."

CHAPTER 01

I DID NOT KNOW

When my family lived in Germany, my mother raised me in the Catholic tradition. The church—with its lofty ceiling, colossal stained-glass windows, gilded altar, and ornate chairs occupied by men in robes—looked like a palace fit for royalty. The Mass, spoken in Latin, left me with a vague concept of God. I returned to America knowing God exists, but I did not know him.

GOD OF JOY AND LAUGHTER

The night I walked into a storefront outreach was the first time I attended a Protestant church service. The interior looked like a home, with the living room furniture replaced by metal chairs and a music stand. I understood the message the young man behind the makeshift pulpit preached: Jesus is returning. We need to be ready.

The only one who returned that night was me. As I prayed, I felt an explosion of joy. The prodigal son,[1] in my case daughter, had come home. In that moment, I became keenly aware of God's presence but did not associate his presence with the institutional church.

Being the middle child in a dysfunctional family had inflicted many emotional wounds. I often cried myself to sleep. After God received me with joy, I still cried when I was alone, but now his presence dried my tears and made me laugh. I knew God existed. I knew there was joy and laughter in his presence, but that was all I knew about God.

PEOPLE WHO KNOW GOD

For months, I walked past a church near my home praying, "Where can I find people who know you?"

One afternoon, a friend and I were riding a tandem bicycle near that church and stopped to rest. She pointed to the church and said, "Do you want to go to church on Sunday?"

The moment I stepped inside the church, I knew I belonged there. They knew more about God than I did and taught me to study the Bible. I learned I had been born again and sealed by God for adoption, which made me his child.[2] But they also taught me a Jekyll-and-Hyde[3] image of the God they worshipped. I knew a God of joy and laughter. They taught me about an abusive tyrant.

The pastor's wife believed God had destroyed her health for his glory. She often boasted about her long list of health problems. The pastor thundered threats from the pulpit. If we didn't spend time with God, we might get in an accident that puts us in the hospital. Then we will have time to pray and read our Bibles.

My experience with God contradicted their theology and filled me with questions. I made an appointment with the pastor. Unable to answer my questions, he abruptly ended the meeting and ushered me out the door. My questions turned me into an unwelcome stranger in the church. I abandoned the church that abandoned me. Instead of asking God for answers, I abandoned him too.

STARTING OVER

Having no marketable job skills, I joined the Air Force. If I had been a man, I would have been packing my bags before the week ended. They put me on the delayed enlistment plan with a departure date in six months.

I stood on the balcony of my apartment, enjoying the warm rays of the sun as I pondered the next chapter of my life. The church had left me disillusioned. I planned to move far away and forget about this God I could not trust.

Thunder interrupted my thoughts. After scanning the clear blue sky with its fluffy white clouds, I assumed I was mistaken. Thunder rumbled again. This time I heard my name.[4] The experience changed me. I started reading the Bible and talking to God again, but wasn't interested in returning to church.

One day, the recruiter called. "You don't want to be in the Air Force," he said. "I'll take care of it."

The unusual statement confused me. I had already taken the oath of office. As I collected my thoughts to respond, he hung up. Since I was legally in the Air Force, I did not believe he could get me out and ignored the call.

When the lease on my apartment ended, I moved home to wait for orders to report for boot camp. Instead, I received an honorable discharge. My hope that the military would give me a job skill paying more than minimum wage vanished. Stuck at home with nowhere to go, I vented my frustration to God.

He responded with a simple command. “Go to church.”

I found emotional healing at my new church. But my questions about God remained unanswered. This time, I brought those questions to God and began a journey to know him. The many conflicting teachings made finding the truth difficult—and sometimes wearisome.

A documentary about Mel Fisher inspired me to continue my quest. Fisher spent over 16 years searching for the legendary Spanish galleon Nuestra Señora de Atocha, which sank in 1622 off the coast of Florida. He often faced criticism from people who doubted he would find the treasure. On July 20, 1985, he proved them wrong. His team discovered the Atocha’s cargo hold, packed with silver bars, emeralds, and gold coins worth hundreds of millions of dollars.

His search for sunken treasure reminded me of passages in Proverbs:

> My son, if you accept my words and store up my commands within you, turning your ear to wisdom and applying your heart to understanding—indeed, if you call out for insight and cry aloud for understanding, and if you look for it as for silver and search for it as for hidden treasure, then you

> will understand the fear of the LORD and find the knowledge of God.—Proverbs 2:1-5

> Blessed are those who find wisdom, those who gain understanding, for she is more profitable than silver and yields better returns than gold. She is more precious than rubies; nothing you desire can compare with her. Long life is in her right hand; in her left hand are riches and honor. Her ways are pleasant ways, and all her paths are peace.—Proverbs 3:13-17

If Fisher could spend more than a decade searching for wealth and find it, I could do the same. He had no guarantee that he would find the treasure he sought. I did. The Bible promises, "If any of you lacks wisdom, you should ask God, who gives generously to all without finding fault, and it will be given to you."[5]

God confirmed he heard my cry for wisdom and understanding during a Sunday morning church service. The pastor walked among his congregation, praying for individuals. Then he walked past me on his way to the pulpit. Suddenly, he stopped, turned around, and walked toward me. He picked up my hand and prayed a simple prayer. "Lord, give her what she has been looking for these many years."

More than a decade later, God fulfilled my desire to know him when a Sunday School superintendent asked me to teach an adult class. As I wrote each lesson, the disconnected pieces of knowledge came together, deepening my understanding of who God is and what he desires to give us.

DISCUSSION QUESTIONS

1. This chapter highlights how easily people can live unaware of God's presence and purpose. Where in your own life do you see signs that you've been living for God without knowing him?

2. When God reveals something new about himself, it often disrupts our assumptions. What assumption about God is challenged in this chapter, and how might embracing the truth change the way you respond to difficult situations?

3. God was working long before the author recognized it. What assurance does that give you about unanswered prayers and long delays?

4. Ignorance of God's character led to fear and confusion. What specific truth about God from this chapter could replace fear with confidence in your current circumstances?

5. What is one practical step you can take this week to live more fully in the truth God has shown you?

CHAPTER 02

THE PROMISE

My quest to know God drew me to the promises he made to Abraham—the father of our faith—after he rescued Lot and the citizens of Sodom from captivity.[6]

When Abraham returned to Sodom with the liberated captives, the king of Sodom said, “Give me the people and keep the goods for yourself.”[7]

But Abraham had sworn an oath to accept nothing belonging to Sodom, lest the king boast that he had made Abraham rich. He took only the provisions his men had consumed during the mission, and the portion of the spoils that rightfully belonged to the men who had assisted him.

After Abraham returned home, God appeared to him in a vision and said, “Do not be afraid, Abram. I am your shield, your very great reward.”[8]

But God had not fulfilled his first promise to give Abraham a son. Ten years after making that promise, Abraham and

Sarah remained childless. He had no reason to believe God and complained about the unfulfilled promise.

"Sovereign LORD, what can you give me since I remain childless and the one who will inherit my estate is Eliezer of Damascus?" And Abraham said, "You have given me no children; so a servant in my household will be my heir." [9]

GOD'S PURPOSE

Abraham wanted to leave his wealth to a son, not a servant. God wanted the same thing. "This man will not be your heir, but a son who is your own flesh and blood will be your heir," said God.[10]

He took Abraham outside and said, "Look now toward heaven, and tell the stars, if thou be able to number them: and he said unto him, so shall thy seed be." [11] One seed according to the apostle Paul, who identified the seed as Jesus.[12]

Abraham and God shared a desire to leave their wealth to a son with one difference. Abraham wanted one son to inherit everything he owned. God wanted a multitude of children so vast they could not be numbered to inherit his wealth with Jesus—his firstborn son.

Adam and Jesus are the only men who do not have a human father. The first Adam, God formed from the dust of the ground, gave us sin and death. The Holy Spirit formed the last Adam, Jesus, in the womb of Mary. Jesus's love for his father did not fail. Adam's love did. Only Jesus can give us eternal life to inherit the eternal kingdom of God because it's fair. How can God give the kingdoms of this world to a sinner and be impartial? Jesus earned the right to rule this planet with his reverent submission, and his love for God and for us.[13]

THE COVENANT

As Abraham gazed at the stars, God repeated his purpose for bringing him to Canaan. "I am the Lord, who brought you out of Ur of the Chaldeans, to give you this land to take possession of it."[14]

Abraham asked a reasonable question. "Sovereign Lord, how can I know that I will gain possession of it?"[15]

God responded by making a covenant with Abraham and sharing the bittersweet truth. Abraham will not possess the land during his lifetime on earth. Then he softened the message with the sweetness of living a long life and dying in peace. There is only one way for Abraham to possess the promised land after he dies. God would have to raise him from the dead.

Jesus told us how Abraham responded that night. "Your father Abraham rejoiced at the thought of seeing my day; he saw it and was glad."[16]

Hebrews Chapter 11 reinforced that concept. "All these people were still living by faith when they died. They did not receive the things promised; they only saw them and welcomed them from a distance, admitting that they were foreigners and strangers on earth."[17] Jesus also died without inheriting the promised land.

The people of faith in Hebrews 11 sought the same thing Abraham wanted. A city with an unshakable foundation, because God is the architect and builder.[18] They longed for a better government than the governments of this world that are easily corrupted by a lust for power to enrich themselves at the expense of the people they rule.[19]

More bitter news followed. Abraham and his descendants will live as foreigners in a land not theirs for four centuries. And a foreign government would oppress his descendants. God balanced that bitterness with a promise to judge the nation that oppressed them and bring his descendants back to the land of promise.

The assurance that Abraham will possess everything God promised through the promised son is the same assurance we have today. The covenant God made to give one of Abraham's sons the land from the river of Egypt to the Euphrates River. On this land, Jesus will establish an incorruptible government that rules all nations on earth with true equality.

THE FULFILLMENT

Abraham's grandson, Jacob, moved his family to Egypt 215 years after Abraham settled in Canaan. The Egyptian government favored them for more than a century. The first generation to live in Egypt would have clung to Abraham's faith. Eventually, their children, who only knew life in Egypt, included Egyptian ideas in their worship and became polytheists.

They were foreigners living on the best land of Egypt when a new regime changed their status with the government from favored to feared.[20] Pharaoh oppressed them because they had become too many for him to control. He feared they would ally themselves with his enemies and leave Egypt.

Their lives grew increasingly bitter when Pharaoh conscripted them to build cities to store his treasure. He tried to reduce their numbers with ruthless treatment by their overseers. When that failed, he ordered his people to kill every newborn male by throwing them into the Nile. The idols of Egypt failed to help Israel, so they cried out to the God of their ancestors.

GOD REMEMBERED

There is one reason God responded to their plight. It is the same reason he responds to ours. He remembered the oath he swore on Mount Moriah when Abraham proved his faith genuine with his actions.[21]

DISCUSSION QUESTIONS

1.God's promises to Abraham were rooted in his character, not Abraham's perfection.

Where in your life do you need to shift your confidence from your own ability to God's faithfulness?

2. God initiated the covenant and carried it forward even when Abraham wavered.

How does knowing that God is the One who sustains his promises change the way you respond to seasons of doubt or weakness?

3. God's promises often unfold slowly and through unexpected paths. What long term prayer in your life requires you to trust God's timing rather than your own expectations?

4. God's promise to bless Abraham ultimately pointed to Jesus and the blessing of salvation for all nations. How does the bigger story of God's redemption help you interpret your present struggles or uncertainties?

5. Abraham acted on God's promise even when he couldn't see the outcome. What is one concrete step of obedience you can take this week that reflects trust in God's character rather than your circumstances?

CHAPTER 03

ISRAEL'S PROBLEM

When God heard the children of Jacob cry for help, he visited Egypt and saw their misery. The misery came from two sources. Egyptian oppression would be the easiest to deal with. The bigger problem lay in the love for idols they inherited from Jacob. The roots of that love ran deep.

A FORGOTTEN VOW

Jacob left his home in Canaan after his mother convinced him to deceive his father and steal his brother's blessing. On his way to Haran (Paddan Aram) to find a wife and escape his brother's wrath, God spoke to him in a dream. [22]In the dream, God confirmed Jacob is the heir to the promises made to Abraham and his seed (Jesus). He also promised to watch over Jacob and bring him back to Canaan.

Jacob woke from the dream and made a vow. If God gave him food, clothes and a safe return to Canaan, he would make Abraham's God his God and give him a tithe of everything he owned.[23] Jacob continued his journey to Haran, where he married Rachel, an idol worshipper, and forgot about his vow.

TIME TO LEAVE

Twenty years later, Jacob had become a wealthy man with a large family. But he no longer felt welcome by Laban, his father-in-law. And Laban's sons are grumbling, "Jacob has taken everything our father owned and has gained all his wealth from what belonged to our father."[24]

As Jacob pondered what to do, God said, "Go back to the land of your fathers and of your relatives, and I will be with you."[25]

Jacob summoned his wives to meet him in the fields for a family discussion. He complained about the way their father cheated him by constantly changing his wages. And there was another important reason they needed to leave. God had appeared to Jacob in a dream and said, "I am the God of Bethel, where you anointed a pillar and where you made a vow to me. Now leave this land at once and go back to your native land."[26] God wanted Jacob to do more than return home. The time had come for Jacob to keep his vow.

Jacob waited for the opportune time to leave without creating a messy confrontation. When Laban left to shear his sheep, Jacob told his wives to pack. Rachel stole the household gods, and they left before Laban returned. Seven days later, Laban caught up with them, angry that Jacob had stolen his gods. But Laban could not find his gods in the camp. They parted peacefully, and Jacob continued the journey to Canaan.

RUNNING FROM GOD

Angels interrupted Jacob's journey. Their presence reminded him of the vow he had no intention of keeping. God had only satisfied two of Jacob's three requirements. If Esau still wanted to kill him, he was not obligated to keep his vow.

He set up camp and sent messengers to his brother in Edom, an eighty-mile trip one way. The round-trip journey would have taken them six to twelve days. In their absence, an angel revealed the source of Jacob's problem. It was customary to place a hand on the thigh during the act of making a vow. The angel touched the hollow of Jacob's thigh, leaving him with a limp as a constant reminder of his broken vow.

The messengers returned with frightening news. Esau was on the way to meet him with 400 men. Jacob was terrified his brother was coming to kill him, but he had nothing to fear. When the small army arrived, Esau "ran to meet Jacob and embraced him; he threw his arms around his neck and kissed him. And they wept."[27] Esau wept tears of joy at seeing his brother again. Jacob wept tears of regret. His last excuse to bypass Bethel dissolved in his brother's arms.

Esau expected Jacob to follow him home for a joyous family reunion. Jacob promised to follow at a slower pace. He could not justify failing to keep his vow, so he ignored it and limped to Shechem instead of Bethel. There he bought a plot of land and pitched his tent. Then had the audacity to set up an altar to El-Elohe-Israel, meaning "God, the God of Israel," a mere twenty miles from Bethel.

Jacob made Abraham's God his God but never fulfilled everything he vowed to do. God's attitude toward those who make vows and do not keep them is clear in Old and New Testament scriptures.

> If you make a vow to the LORD your God, do not be slow to pay it, for the LORD your God will certainly demand it of you, and you will be guilty of sin. ... Whatever your lips utter you must be sure to do, because you made your vow freely to the LORD your God with your own mouth.—Deuteronomy 23:21, 23

> When you make a vow to God, do not delay to fulfill it. He has no pleasure in fools; fulfill your vow. It is better not to make a vow than to make one and not fulfill it. Do not let your mouth lead you into sin. And do not protest to the temple messenger, "My vow was a mistake." Why should God be angry at what you say and destroy the work of your hands?—Ecclesiastes 5:4-6

> But I tell you, do not swear an oath at all: either by heaven, for it is God's throne; or by the earth, for it is his footstool; or by Jerusalem, for it is the city of the Great King. And do not swear by your head, for you cannot make even one hair white or black. All you need to say is simply 'Yes' or 'No'; anything beyond this comes from the evil one.—Matthew 5:34-37

God reminded Jacob of his vow. Jacob responded by returning to Canaan and skipping Bethel. Five years after settling in Shechem, God allowed the works of his hands to be destroyed. Shechem, son of Hamor, raped his daughter. His sons deceived Hamor, the ruler of the city, into an agreement they had no intention of keeping.

The men of the city kept the one requirement, circumcision, for them to unite with Jacob's family. Three days later, when the men were in pain, Simon and Levi slaughtered every man in the city, including Hamor and Shechem. Then all the sons of Jacob looted the city.

THE STRUGGLE TO OVERCOME

Jacob rebuked his sons. No one in the area would ever do business with him again. He was terrified that the surrounding cities would unite and take revenge on his family. God had told Jacob that he would be with him wherever he went and kept his word. During the tragedy, he gave Jacob the solution. "Go up to Bethel and settle there, and build an altar there to God, who appeared to you when you were fleeing from your brother Esau."[28]

God had patiently waited twenty-five years for Jacob to fulfill his vow. Jacob was not willing to keep his word until he suffered the consequences of failing to keep his vow. Circumstances forced him to Bethel.

Jacob had a lukewarm relationship with God. He tolerated Rachel's theft of her father's idols. The worship of false idols had co-existed in his family with the worship of the God of Abraham for decades. God's love and faithfulness eventually moved Jacob to rid his home of idol worship.

He commanded his household to "Get rid of the foreign gods you have with you and purify yourselves, and change your clothes. Then come, let us go up to Bethel, where I will build an altar to God, who answered me in the day of my distress and who has been with me wherever I have gone."[29]

Jacob cleansed his house of the symbols of idol worship, but not their hearts, including his heart. He hid the idols under the oak of Shechem. Why didn't Jacob destroy them? Hiding the idols left the door open for him to retrieve them. Many years later, Joshua stood under the oak of Shechem and commanded Isreal to destroy their idols.[30]

The idol worship Jacob hid remained in his descendants and flourished again when they moved to Egypt.

Jacob wrestled with his character and devotion to God all his life. His descendants became like him. They also struggled with their love of idols in Egypt, in the wilderness, and when judges and kings ruled them. With some exceptions, they never made Abraham's God their one and only God. And without exception, God never failed to love and help them.

DISCUSSION QUESTIONS

1. Jacob often tried to secure God's blessings through his own schemes. Do you see that same impulse in your own life? Instead of trusting God, have you tried to help him only to create trouble in your life?

2. God patiently pursued Jacob, even when Jacob resisted surrender. How does God's persistence with Jacob challenge the way you interpret God's patience toward your own stubborn choices?

3. Jacob's family inherited his mixture of faith and fear. What have you inherited — spiritually or emotionally — that God may be inviting you to confront rather than pass down?

4. When Jacob finally faced God honestly, transformation began. Are you wrestling with God instead submitting to his way?

5. Israel repeated Jacob's mistakes because they knew God's promises but didn't trust his character. What promise of God do you believe intellectually but struggle to rely on in daily life?

CHAPTER 04

EGYPT'S PROBLEM

The existence of humanity began with the truth about God. Adam and Eve lacked what their offspring would possess—childhood memories. There was nothing in their past to distort the knowledge they possessed about God. He taught them the truth about their origins and provided them with everything they needed. He also warned them about the danger of eating from the tree of knowledge of good and evil. Unfortunately, they chose evil.

SPREAD OF PAGAN THEOLOGY

Adam and Eve's rebellion filled the world with violence and prompted God's decision to start over. Everyone died in a flood except Noah's family. His descendants settled on the plains of Shinar, where his great-grandson, Nimrod, convinced many they did not need God to be happy. They were one family with one language, following a man who thought he was wiser than the God who created them.

Christian and Jewish traditions point to Nimrod as the creator of institutional idolatry.[31] His theology allowed for many gods from which he derived his authority to rule.

Nimrod led them to build a city and tower where he could ascend to heaven and take revenge on God for killing their ancestors.[32]

God ended Nimrod's plans when he confused their language and scattered them. The people brought Nimrod's theology with them and built small cities. Each city had a local deity, sacred animal or emblem, and a chief who acted as a representative of the deity.

ROOTS OF EGYPT

Egypt was born when several of the cities near the Nile River united. Their religion provided them authority to rule. Government gave them the tools to enforce their beliefs on their citizens. Eventually, religion and government became so intertwined that government itself functioned as a religious institution. The king became the mediator between the gods and humans. His primary duty became *ma'at*—cosmic order, justice, and balance. The people revered his commands as expressions of God's will, which made obedience a moral obligation. Disobedience became a violation of the cosmic order, and government projects became a religious duty.

Temples became more than places of worship. They became economic centers, controlling land and labor. The priests and scribes performed the administrative duties of the government, and preserved their myths, rituals, and sacred knowledge. Religion grew so powerful that it touched every aspect of governance.

JOSEPH'S ARRIVAL

Joseph's arrival in Egypt and subsequent exaltation by Pharaoh, after he interpreted Pharaoh's dream, made

Pharaoh all-powerful. Joseph did more than foretell seven years of plenty followed by a severe seven-year famine. He offered a solution. Pharaoh gave Joseph the power to implement the solution so Egypt would survive the famine.

Before the famine ended, Egypt collected all the money in Egypt and Cannan selling the grain Joseph had stockpiled. The people had no money, so they sold all their livestock to Egypt for food. With nothing left to buy grain, they sold their land and themselves into slavery.

The famine brought Joseph's family to Egypt, where they remained after the famine ended. His position in Egypt gave them the best land in Goshen, and a shield of protection from any who would harm them. They prospered and multiplied, but never treated as equals. They were shepherds, an occupation the Egyptians despised for religious reasons.

SEPARATE FROM CHRIST

The Egyptians "were separate from Christ, excluded from citizenship in Israel and were foreigners to the covenants of the promise, without hope and without God in the world."[33] But that is not how Egypt began. They were not heirs of God's promises, but they knew the truth about God.

Egyptologist Sir E. A. Wallis Budge opened the first chapter of *Egyptian Ideas of the Future Life* with a firm conviction about the foundation of Egyptian religion.

> "A study of ancient Egyptian religious texts will convince the reader that the Egyptians believed in One God, who was self-existent, immortal, invisible, eternal, omniscient, almighty, and inscrutable; the

maker of the heavens, earth, and underworld; the creator of the sky and the sea, men and women, animals and birds, fish and creeping things, trees and plants, and the incorporeal beings who were the messengers that fulfilled his wish and word. It is necessary to place this definition of the first part of the belief of the Egyptian at the beginning of the first chapter of this brief account of the principal religious ideas which he held, for the whole of his theology and religion was based upon it."[34]

Budge rejects the idea that immigrants from the East brought this concept to Egypt. He acknowledged the Egyptians became polytheistic but insists that the foundation of their religious ideas from their earliest manuscripts maintains their belief in one God, creator of all things, and that belief continued throughout their existence.

The Apostle Paul explained the source of the Egyptians' and Israelites' polytheism in his letter to the Romans. The leaders of Egypt and Israel knew the truth and suppressed it.

> "For since the creation of the world God's invisible qualities—his eternal power and divine nature—have been clearly seen being understood from what has been made, so that people are without excuse. For although they knew God, they neither glorified him as God nor gave thanks to him, but their thinking became futile, and their foolish hearts were darkened. Although they claimed to be wise, they became fools and exchanged the glory of the immortal God for images made to look like mortal human beings and birds and animals and reptiles." [35]

The Egyptians drifted into error, and the Israelites followed them. Both worshiped idols. Both taught and obeyed human commands, making their worship of the one true God vain.[36]

Egypt and the Israelites started with the same concept of God, with one difference. The covenants of promise that impart hope belonged to the Israelites. Instead of the Israelites influencing the Egyptians' beliefs, they embraced Egypt's theology. They started their life in Egypt as despised shepherds. In a quest for equality, they shed their shepherds' cloaks to become co-laborers with Egyptians to build Pharaoh's treasure cities. Egypt never accepted them as equals, and their labor became slavery. God was not willing that anyone should perish, and everyone in Egypt had lost their way.

DISCUSSION QUESTIONS

1. How does the chapter's explanation of Egypt's spiritual blindness help you recognize areas in your own life where you may be unaware of false doctrines?

2. God confronted Egypt not to destroy them but to reveal Himself. Where have you mistaken God's correction for punishment?

3. Egypt trusted its own wisdom, power, and traditions instead of God. What sources of security do you tend to rely on, and what would it look like to shift your trust back to God?

4. God exposes the real problem so he can bring real deliverance. What truth about yourself or your situation has God revealed? Why should you cooperate with him instead of resisting?

5. God's purposes move forward even when people misunderstand him. How does this encourage you when you feel unsure of what God is doing?

CHAPTER 05

THE SOLUTION

God had an unexpected solution for Egypt and Israel's problems. He appeared to Moses, who did not need help, to send him to Pharaoh, who was not asking for help.

ARISE FROM SLEEP

Paul explained why God dealt with Pharaoh before he delivered the Israelites. In his letter to the Romans, he quoted God's message to Pharaoh, "I raised you up for this very purpose, that I might display my power in you and that my name might be proclaimed in all the earth."[37] Paul used a Greek word for raised that means to arouse from sleep.[38]

God had more than the ancient Egyptians and Israelites on his mind. He endured Pharaoh's arrogance to benefit "all the earth" by making his love and mercy known to everyone. Love does no wrong to a neighbor. God went to Egypt to love Pharaoh by waking him from spiritual sleep and educating him to the truth about the idols of Egypt, so everyone on earth can know the truth about God. Then Paul concluded, "God has mercy on whom he wants to have mercy, and he hardens whom he wants to harden."[39]

HARDENING

Some believe God hardened Pharaoh's heart so he could destroy him and all of Egypt. That belief contradicts God's character. The Bible defines God as love. Would God who takes no pleasure in the death of the wicked, deny them a way to escape the consequences of their sin?[40]

In the account of the Israelites' deliverance from Egypt's power, three Hebrew words—*chazaq*, *kabad*, and *qashah*, are translated hard or harden. Each word carries a different meaning.

Chazaq means to make strong, courageous, strengthen, cure, help, repair.[41] It describes the physical and moral strength God gives us to believe. We can use that strength to obey him or turn that strength into stubbornness against him.

Kabad means heavy, in a good sense meaning numerous or in a bad sense meaning difficult or stupid.[42] Our hearts can become heavy with numerous reasons to believe in God's love. But if we close our eyes to the truth, it makes us difficult to deal with and we make stupid decisions.

Qashah means to be dense, tough, or severe. It is similar in meaning to *kabad* and only used once in God's dealings with Pharaoh. *Kabad* is what fools do with *chazaq* (the strength to believe). The mercy of God can harden us into a stubborn Abraham, who believed the best of God when circumstances said otherwise. But ignoring mercy can also turn us into a foolish Pharaoh. Pharaoh experienced God's goodness when God gave him credible, verifiable evidence to believe and obey him. Pharaoh responded to that evidence with a stubborn refusal to obey God. If we repeatedly *kabad* our hearts against the truth, our hearts become *qashah* (dense).

All God's dealings with Pharaoh were designed to return the Egyptians to the truth they had abandoned so they could live. A commentary on Pharaoh's heart follows each miracle he witnessed. Either God strengthened Pharaoh's heart by giving him reasons to believe, or Pharaoh's heart became *kabad*, heavy with the truth he refused to accept.

GOD'S JUSTICE

To those who question God's justice in his dealings with Pharaoh, Paul pointed to God's rights as a potter by using an example from Jeremiah chapter 18.[43] God sent Jeremiah to the potter's house to watch the potter form a vessel. When the vessel crafted by the potter on the wheel was marred, he reshaped it into a new form.

God told Jeremiah, as the clay is in the potter's hand, so are the nations on earth in God's hands. If he decides to destroy a nation for its evil, but that nation repents, he will reshape it into a vessel filled with his blessings. If God blesses a nation, but that nation does evil in his sight and refuses to obey his voice, he will destroy that nation. When God came to Egypt to deliver the Israelites, he put Egypt's leaders on the potter's wheel. If they had repented by granting God's request to let Israel go into the wilderness and worship him, he would have remade them into a vessel filled with his blessings.

THE WILL OF GOD

Paul wrote to the Galatians Jesus "gave himself for our sins to rescue us from the present evil age, according to the will of our God and Father."[44] From Adam and Eve's sin and expulsion from the garden to this day, there has always been a remnant who believed in one God and looked forward to the coming of the promised seed (Jesus). Waiting is hard. We often drift from the truth, as Egypt and Israel did.

Today, we are still waiting, as we live by faith in an evil age. God's people are still living as Abraham and all the heroes of faith did—strangers and foreigners.[45] One day, according to the will of God, Jesus's reign will replace the governments of this age with true justice and equality for all.

DISCUSSION QUESTIONS

1. This chapter shows God providing a solution no one expected. Where in your life are you limiting God to the solutions you can imagine, and how might trusting him change your outlook?

2. God's answer to Israel's suffering involved raising up Moses long before the people cried out. What does this teach us about God's timing, and where do you need to trust that he has already begun working ahead of your need?

3. God's solutions often confront human pride and assumptions. What belief might God be challenging in you as part of his solution to a current struggle?

4. God's solution required Moses to obey even when he felt inadequate. What step of obedience is God asking you to take that feels uncomfortable?

5. God's solution is always rooted in his covenant love. How would your daily decisions shift if you truly believed God is committed to your good even when his path feels difficult?

CHAPTER 06

THE CALLING

Moses' parents, Amram and Jochebed, were among the remnant who remained faithful to Abraham's God. When Pharaoh decreed the death of the male Israelite children, they were not afraid even though they had reason to fear.[46] If any Israelite family let their newborn son live, the entire family would be killed.[47]

Amram and Jochebed committed the fate of their youngest son, Moses, to God. They made a basket and set the three-month-old infant among the reeds of the Nile. God rewarded their fearless faith when Pharaoh's daughter found the baby and paid Jochebed to nurse him.

FAITH

Moses became the privileged grandson of Pharaoh for forty years. But Egypt never destroyed the faith Amram and Jochebed instilled in Moses. He thought his own people would understand that God had called him to deliver them from the oppression of Egypt.[48] When he saw an Egyptian beating a Hebrew, he killed the Egyptian and hid the body. The next day, he saw two Israelites fighting and sought to reconcile them. The Israelite doing wrong pushed him away and said, "Who made you ruler and judge over us? Are you thinking of killing me as you killed the Egyptian yesterday?"[49]

The Israelite man who suffered at the hands of the abusive Egyptian was the only one who knew Moses had killed the Egyptian. How did Pharaoh know what happened unless the man Moses rescued from abuse told other Israelites and an Israelite told the government of Egypt.[50] Pharaoh already feared the Israelites would turn against him and leave. He could not tolerate Moses, the adopted Israelite grandson of his predecessor, educated in all the wisdom of the Egyptians and mighty in words and deeds, acting like a ruler and judge of the Israelites.[51]

Circumstances forced Moses out of Egypt, not fear. Moses's effort to help his people revealed they would not accept him as their ruler. Pharaoh and his officials wanted him dead. He could not help people who did not want his help. The hearts of the Israelites belonged to Egypt. Moses's heart belonged to God.

Moses abandoned the idol-worshipping Israelites in Egypt to start a new life in Midian as a free man. Like Abraham before him, Moses confessed he was a stranger in this world.[52] He endured their rejection because he saw Jesus's day as did Abraham before him, and all the great people of faith after him did.[53]

THE CALL

Moses had been living as a shepherd for forty years when he led his flock to the far side of the wilderness.

An intriguing sight caught his eye: a fruit-bearing thorn bush on fire that was not being consumed.[54] He drew near to investigate.

When God saw he had Moses's attention, he called him by name and said, "Do not come any closer. Take off your sandals, for the place where you are standing is holy ground."[55] Then he identified himself as the God of Abraham, Isaac, and Jacob. Moses had entered the presence of Abraham's God, who promised to bring his descendants back to the land of Canaan.

I HAVE SEEN

Moses feared to look upon God and hid his face as he listened. "I have indeed seen the misery of my people in Egypt. I have heard them crying out because of their slave drivers, and I am concerned about their suffering. So, I have come down to rescue them from the hand of the Egyptians and to bring them up out of that land into a good and spacious land, a land flowing with milk and honey...And now the cry of the Israelites has reached me, and I have seen the way the Egyptians are oppressing them. So now, go. I am sending you to Pharaoh to bring my people, the Israelites, out of Egypt." [56]

Time had destroyed Moses's desire to fulfill his calling. But the sting of rejection never faded. Moses objected. He had already tried to help his people. The Israelites refused to recognize his God-given authority. If they did not believe him, why would Pharaoh?

God replied, "I will be with you. And this will be the sign to you it is I who have sent you. When you have brought the people out of Egypt, you will worship God on this mountain." [57]

Moses would know that the God of his ancestors spoke the truth when he worshipped God on the mountain with the children of those who rejected him. God also made a distinction in the part each of them would fulfill. God will bring Israel into the land he promised to Abraham and his seed (Jesus). Moses will bring them out of Egypt to worship God on the mountain. He never said Moses would bring them into the promised land.

WHAT IF

Moses was afraid to look at God, but not afraid to argue with him. "What if they ask me what your name is?"

"Tell them *'I AM'* sent me to you, said God."[58] Then he repeated the name he already gave Moses. He is the God of Abraham, Isaac, and Jacob.

God assured Moses the elders of Israel would believe him and told Moses what would happen in Egypt. When Moses and the elders request a leave of absence to worship their God, Pharaoh will say no.

Moses began his "what if" scenario again. "What if they do not believe me or listen to me and say, 'The Lord did not appear to you'?"[59]

God gave Moses three signs so the Israelite elders would have more evidence than Moses's word to believe their ancestors God appeared to him. He told Moses to throw his shepherd's staff on the ground. It became a snake. Moses took the snake by its tail, and it became a staff again.

If they did not believe that sign, Moses could put his hand inside his cloak. When he withdrew his hand, it would be leprous. He would heal his hand by putting it inside his cloak and withdrawing it. If they did not believe those signs, Moses could take water from the Nile. When he pours the water on the ground, it will be blood.

As a grandson of Pharaoh, Moses had seen the Egyptian priests turn rods into serpents and water into blood. Unimpressed with the signs—and the fact he had a major role to play in fulfilling God's promises to Abraham—he educated God about who he was talking to.

"Pardon your servant, Lord. I have never been eloquent, neither in the past nor since you have spoken to your servant. I am slow of speech and tongue." [60]

Moses feared to look upon God but was not afraid to lie to him. During the time he lived as Pharaoh's grandson, he was known as powerful in speech and action.[61] Moses's objections were lame excuses to avoid fulfilling his calling.

THE TRUTH

God never condemned Moses for lying to him. He educated Moses about whom Moses was talking to. The great I AM informed Moses that he was talking to the creator who gave Moses a mouth. Then he said, "Now go; I will help you speak and will teach you what to say."[62]

Moses had run out of excuses, so he confessed the truth. "Pardon your servant, Lord. Please send someone else." [63] Moses' desire to fulfill God's calling had died. He did not want to be a ruler and judge over people who rejected him.

His attitude angered God. He could have killed Moses or rejected him to choose someone else. Instead, he loved

Moses by bearing his weakness. He appointed Aaron to speak for Moses as if Moses were a god[64] and Aaron his prophet. God promised to be with both men and teach Moses what to do.[65]

DISCUSSION QUESTIONS

1. God was already at work in Moses' life long before Moses understood his calling. Where can you now recognize God preparing you in ways you didn't appreciate at the time, and how does that change your confidence in Him today?

2. God's call came to Moses while he was living an ordinary life in Midian. What does this teach you about God's ability to use seasons when you feel overlooked, and how might that change how you view your current season?

3. Moses resisted God's call because he focused on his limitations. What limitation or weakness do you tend to fixate on? What can you do to focus on God's sufficiency instead of your inadequacy?

4. God revealed His heart, His name, and His purpose before asking Moses to obey. How does knowing who God is give you courage to take the next step of obedience in your own life?

5. Moses' calling was ultimately about God's mission, not Moses' comfort. What is one area where you sense God inviting you to align your life more fully with His purpose, even if it stretches you beyond what feels comfortable?

CHAPTER 07

THE REVIVAL

Moses's return to Egypt started a revival. The elders of Israel assembled their congregations for a joint meeting in Goshen. Aaron preached and performed the signs God gave Moses, so the people would have a reason to believe them. The Israelites believed that their ancestors' God had come to help them, and they worshipped him.[66] But their worship was not sincere.

GOD'S PERSPECTIVE

Centuries after God delivered the Israelites from Egypt, their government collapsed, and they were taken into captivity. Some elders asked Ezekiel to inquire of God for them. God told Ezekiel why he refused to speak to them.

> "On the day I chose Israel, I swore with uplifted hand to the descendants of Jacob and revealed myself to them in Egypt. With uplifted hand I said to them, 'I am the Lord your God.' On that day I swore to them I would bring them out of Egypt into a land I had searched out for them, a land flowing with milk and honey, the

> most beautiful of all lands. And I said to them, 'Each of you, get rid of the vile images you have set your eyes on, and do not defile yourselves with the idols of Egypt. I am the Lord your God.' But they rebelled against me and would not listen to me; they did not get rid of the vile images they had set their eyes on, nor did they forsake the idols of Egypt." [67]

God made more than a promise of deliverance during the revival. He gave them a light burden and easy yoke—make him their one and only God.[68]

PHARAOH DID NOT KNOW

The people who needed deliverance did not have to deal with Pharaoh. God had already prepared Moses, who did not need deliverance, to deal with their oppressor. All Israel had to do was wait while God destroyed the lies that made them willing slaves of a religious tyrant.

In *Exploring Exodus*, the observation is made that, "... the request for temporary relief from drudgery in order to celebrate a religious holiday was not something unreasonable or exceptional in the Egyptian system of state-imposed servitude." [69]

Moses, Aaron, and the elders entered Pharaoh's throne room to make a common request.[70] Aaron delivered God's message. "This is what the Lord, the God of Israel, says: "Let my people go, so that they may hold a festival to me in the wilderness." [71]

Pharaoh replied, "Who is the LORD, that I should obey him and let Israel go? I do not know the LORD and I will not let Israel go." [72]

The Egyptians revered Pharaoh as a living god on earth. He governed with absolute authority. As high priest of every temple, the Egyptians expected him to keep their idols happy, lest they bring disaster upon their nation. The over 2,000 idols worshipped in Egypt rose and fell in prominence at the ruling Pharaoh's whims. Allowing the worship of a God he did not know jeopardized his control over their religion, which he used to control the nation.[73]

Did God, who created the planet we live on and gave us life, need the permission of a mere human? Why would God ask Pharaoh's permission to let Israel go into the wilderness and worship?

Jesus shed light on God's treatment of Pharaoh when he said, "Let me teach you, because I am humble and gentle at heart."[74] God could have humiliated Pharaoh or killed him. Instead, he came to Pharaoh with respect for his position and worked within the laws of Egypt to take his people into the wilderness peacefully.

GOD'S MINISTERS DID NOT KNOW

Not content with Pharaoh's "NO," the Israelite delegation repeated their request with an appeal to Pharaoh's goodness. "The God of the Israelites has met with us. Now let us take a three-day journey into the wilderness to offer sacrifices to the Lord our God, or he may strike us with plagues or with the sword."[75] Pharaoh was not the only one in the meeting who did not know God. Why did God's ministers think he would destroy them with pestilence or with the sword? He had already told Moses that Pharaoh would refuse to let them leave.

Everyone in this meeting of religious leaders knew about God, but they did not know God. Abraham's God came to Egypt to keep the promises he made to Jesus, Abraham, Isaac and Jacob. The Egyptians were the only ones in jeopardy of plagues and death if their Pharaoh denied God's request to let his people worship him in the wilderness.

DISCUSSION QUESTIONS

1. What does the "revival" in Egypt reveal about the difference between emotional belief and true repentance?

2. How did God's command to make him their one and only God contrast with the heavy burdens Pharaoh placed on Israel?

3. What does the idea that God was destroying "the lies that made them willing slaves" say about the process of deliverance?

4. Why would God choose to approach Pharaoh respectfully even though he had greater power and authority? What does that teach us about God's character?

5. How did Moses and the elders fear they might be struck with plagues or the sword if they didn't worship God show us the difference between knowing about God and knowing God?

CHAPTER 08

THE BATTLE FOR TRUTH

Oblivious to the Israelites' misery, Pharaoh sought to sway the elders against Moses and Aaron by pointing to the condition of the Israelites. "Look, the people of the land are now many, and you are stopping them from working," said Pharoah.[76] Then he dismissed the Israelite delegation to go back to work.

THE FIRST SPEAR

After Moses, Aaron, and the elders left, Pharaoh did more than deny their request. Moses, a former prince of Egypt, had returned with a mission. Convince the Israelites to worship God according to his religious convictions. Feeling threatened by the appearance of a new god he did not know, Pharaoh threw the first spear at Moses by calling him a liar.

He commanded the Egyptian taskmasters to tell the Israelite officers Egypt would no longer supply straw for making bricks.[77] "They are lazy; that is why they are crying out, 'Let us go and sacrifice to our God.' Make the work harder for the people so that they keep working and pay no attention to lies."[78]

DID MOSES LIE

In hindsight, we know the Israelites Moses led out of Egypt never returned. Did Moses lie when he said they were only going into the wilderness to worship God?

No.

First, God made the request. It is impossible for God to lie.[79] Second, they never left the wilderness. Even after their children crossed the Jordan River to establish a temporary occupation of the land, they remained in a spiritual wilderness. From the time God arrived in Egypt to deliver them to the time they ceased to exist as a nation, with some exceptions, they never forsook worshiping the idols of Egypt. God will not share his glory with others.[80] Only those who worship God alone receive the fulfillment of his promises.

IRRATIONAL DEMAND

The Israelite officers[81] who worked for Egypt delivered the irrational demand to produce the same quota of bricks without the government supplying the straw. When they failed to fulfill the quota, the officers who led their nation into the service of Pharaoh were beaten.[82] A daily quota—impossible to fulfill—meant a daily beating. The injustice of the demand and abusive treatment brought the Israelites face-to-face with the truth about Pharaoh and exposed the insincerity of the Israelites' worship.

The officers made an appointment with Pharaoh to complain about their Egyptian taskmasters. "Why have you treated your servants this way? Your servants are given no straw, yet we are told, 'Make bricks!' Your servants are being beaten, but the fault is with your own people."[83]

Their hope of fair treatment shattered in the angry blast of Pharaoh's reply: "Lazy, that's what you are—lazy! That is why you keep saying, 'Let us go and sacrifice to the Lord.' Now get to work. You will not be given any straw, yet you must produce your full quota of bricks."[84]

The officers left Pharaoh's presence to blame Moses and Aaron for their predicament. "May the Lord look on you and judge you! You have made us obnoxious to Pharaoh and his officials and have put a sword in their hand to kill us."[85]

They made themselves obnoxious to God when they cried for justice from Pharaoh and called themselves his servants three times. The officers created their problem when they cried out to their father's God for help but never did the one thing he asked of them: make him their one and only God.

FAITH SHAKEN

Pharaoh's strategy to turn the Israelites against Moses almost worked. The officers' accusation shook Moses's faith. He prayed, "Why, Lord, have you brought trouble on this people? Is this why you sent me? Ever since I went to Pharaoh to speak in your name, he has brought trouble on this people, and you have not rescued your people at all."[86]

Moses's questions came from a lack of knowledge. He did not hear the officers call themselves Pharaoh's servants three times, but God did. They worshipped God and wanted to be free from misery, but their hearts belonged to Pharaoh. They thought Pharaoh would be fair and protect them, only to learn Pharaoh was not the fair and benevolent ruler they thought he was. The officers blamed Pharaoh's officials for their misery, but it was Pharaoh who made it impossible to fulfill the quota. They left Pharaoh angry with Moses and Aaron because they had fallen out of favor with the tyrant who made their lives miserable.

Shouldn't they have been angry with Pharaoh?

Giving us a better life is easy for God to do. He gives disobedient people a better life, because his goodness leads us to repentance. But it's hard to obey God until we know the truth that sets us free. Sometimes the source of our misery is our love for people in authority who know about God but do not know God, and do not love us.

When God is called upon to right an injustice, his judgments begin with his own people. Those who lead receive stricter judgments.[87] The Israelites who cried out to God for help were no better than their oppressors. They wanted God to make Pharaoh treat them fairly, so serving Pharaoh would be easier.

Allowing Pharaoh to treat Israel evil should have opened their eyes. It should have provoked them to say, "Why are we serving Pharaoh? He made our job impossible and will not stop his people from beating us for our failure to fulfill his unreasonable demand." Why didn't they cry out, "We've had enough of Pharaoh's harsh, hateful ways?"

OUR FATHER

Sometimes our suffering is self-inflicted and deserved. The leaders of Israel multiplied their misery when they refused to accept the light and easy burden of making their ancestors' God their one and only God. Trouble comes upon everyone who does evil.[88] If we love the tyrants in this world more than God, who loves us, trouble will come upon us.

God had a broader intent than delivering a disobedient people who abandoned him to serve a tyrant. He wanted his power over the tyrants who rule us to be declared throughout the earth.[89] The trouble that came upon the Israelites should have given them the ability to see the truth about God and human rulers.

Instead, the officers wanted God to judge Moses and Aaron for making them abhorrent to the Egyptians and putting a sword in their hand to kill them.[90] Blowing things out of proportion is a characteristic of immaturity. That wasn't a sword in the Egyptians' hands. It was the whip of God's discipline. The disobedient officers who led their nation astray only got a spanking because their Father in heaven loved them.[91]

DISCUSSION QUESTIONS

1. How does Pharaoh's tactic of increasing suffering to control belief show the way oppressive systems work today?

2. How does the chapter's claim that Israel "never left the wilderness" spiritually challenge common assumptions about the Exodus?

3. What did Israel's persistent idolatry reveal about the difference between physical deliverance and spiritual obedience?

4. What does the officer's expectation of fairness from Pharaoh reveal about the human tendency to trust oppressive authorities?

5. What "tyrants" in your own life have you trusted more than God?

CHAPTER 09

I WAS NOT KNOWN

God responded to Moses's complaint that trouble had come upon Israel instead of deliverance by pointing to the future.[92] The Israelites wanted a better life in Egypt as Pharaoh's servants. God wanted to keep the promises he made to Jesus, Abraham, Isaac, and Jacob. He started with Abraham's family, but he never intended for his blessings to belong to one family. He wants everyone included in his blessings of an eternal, incorruptible king to rule us with righteous and justice for all.

REVELATION

God said to Moses, "I am Lord. I appeared to Abraham, to Isaac, and to Jacob as God Almighty, but by my name the Lord, I did not make myself fully known to them."[93]

God's names reveal who he is. The patriarchs knew him as God Almighty (El Shaddai), the God who multiplies us into a multitude.[94] They did not know him as Lord. When God kept his promise to judge their oppressors, he taught the Israelites who had strayed from their faith that the God Almighty of their forefathers is also Lord.[95]

The revelations God gives to each generation build on the knowledge he gave to previous generations. As he adds knowledge to the knowledge we already have, it paints a clearer picture of the God we worship. That knowledge belongs to us and to our children forever.[96]

YOU ARE MINE AND I AM YOURS

God said to Moses, "I will take you as my own people, and I will be your God."[97] The fulfillment of God's desire to dwell among a people who know and love him takes place after the first heaven and earth pass away.

The Apostle John saw the day God will dwell among us in the New Jerusalem and recorded that event in Revelation.

> "Then I saw "a new heaven and a new earth," for the first heaven and the first earth had passed away, and there was no longer any sea. I saw the Holy City, the new Jerusalem, coming down out of heaven from God, prepared as a bride beautifully dressed for her husband. And I heard a loud voice from the throne saying, "Look! God's dwelling place is now among the people, and he will dwell with them. They will be his people, and God himself will be with them and be their God. 'He will wipe every tear from their eyes. There will be no more death, or mourning, or crying, or pain, for the old order of things has passed away." Revelation 21:1-3

GOD'S INTENTION

Paul shed additional light on God's intentions in his letter to the Romans.

> "What if God, although choosing to show his wrath and make his power known, bore with great patience the objects of his wrath—prepared for destruction? What if he did this to make the riches of his glory known to the objects of his mercy, whom he prepared in advance for glory—even us, whom he also called, not only from the Jews but also from the Gentiles?" Romans 9:22-24

The vessels of mercy are both Jews and Gentiles.[98] God went to Egypt to show how merciful and patient he can be by treating everyone in Egypt with compassion. Everyone is a vessel of wrath prepared for destruction. Everyone can become a vessel of mercy prepared for glory.[99] There is one reason some become vessels of God's wrath. They mock his mercy like Pharaoh and his servants who knew the truth about God and refused to let Israel worship him.

OUR CHOICE

The tyrants of this world are God's problem. He performed miraculous signs and wonders in Egypt that proved he is greater than Pharaoh and Egypt's false religion, so the people who submitted to Pharaoh would have a choice. We can cling to the tyrants we love and perish with them. Or we can be free to serve a God whose love for us is genuine.

Moses delivered God's message of love to the elders. They will be his people, and he will be their God. But God's discipline made them so miserable they did not want to hear it. How we respond to the truth God reveals to us is our choice. The truth is a double-edged sword that can set us free from tyrants who abuse us, or justify God when he destroys tyrants and their followers who enable the abusive tyrant to reign.

DISCUSSION QUESTIONS

1. What does God's desire to dwell among his people reveal about his heart and his priorities?

2. What does it reveal about God that He "bore with great patience the objects of His wrath?"

3. What distinguishes a vessel of mercy from a vessel of wrath?

4. How do God's signs and wonders in Egypt show his desire to give people a choice?

5. How does the image of truth as a double-edged sword encourage us to accept the truth God reveals?

CHAPTER 10

HE IS LORD

Pharaoh's lack of knowledge about God created his problems.[100] He believed Moses was a liar and a troublemaker. Egypt needed Israel to do the hard, dirty work of making bricks to build cities, so Pharaoh would have a place to store his treasures. Pharaoh needed to discredit Moses and Aaron, so Israel would forget about worshipping their ancestors' God and keep making bricks.

MAGICIANS

God said to Moses, "When Pharaoh says to you, 'Perform a miracle,' then say to Aaron, 'Take your staff and throw it down before Pharaoh,' and it will become a snake."[101] Jesus said, "A wicked and adulterous generation asks for a miraculous sign."[102]

Aaron cast down his staff, and it became a serpent. Unimpressed, Pharaoh summoned the Lector Priests. They were ritual specialists and guardians of secret knowledge, known for their ability to alter reality with spells and hidden wisdom.[103]

Pharaoh used religion deceitfully to manipulate his followers. He assumed Moses and Aaron were doing the same thing. According to Josephus, a first-century Jewish historian, Pharaoh told Moses he was not the only person who knew how to do these tricks. Only the ignorant would believe God turned the rod into a snake.[104] Then the magicians threw down their rods, which also became serpents.[105]

They did not expect God's serpent would challenge their religious authority by swallowing their serpents. Aaron's staff, which became a living snake, would have been viewed as a foreign divine power invading a domain the priest believed they controlled. The scene of a magic greater than theirs would have been shocking to the priest.[106]

God's message to Egypt was clear. Their idols cannot protect them. Moses and Aaron had not lied as Pharaoh claimed. God exists; he possesses superior power, and he wants Pharaoh to let the Israelites go into the wilderness to worship him.

A shepherd's staff turning into a serpent is a sign God gave to Moses so people would believe him. The Israelites saw the signs first. Those who had not asked for a sign welcomed the truth and worshiped God.

Pharaoh asked for a miraculous sign to prove his claim that Moses and Aaron were liars. Instead, he witnessed a credible reason to believe they told the truth. Pharaoh willfully closed his eyes to the truth that could set him free, so he could maintain the status quo.

DENYING THE TRUTH

That evening God told Moses Pharaoh's heart is kābēd (dull, stupid). Pharaoh had denied God's request to let the Israelites worship him because he did not know the Lord. God responded by making himself and his power known. Pharaoh and his religious leaders witnessed God's superior authority, but they did not change their minds. Pharaoh refused to grant Israel religious freedom.

BLOOD

God responded to Pharaoh's stubbornness with mercy by giving him another reason to believe and obey him. He told Moses to bring the staff—that represented a reason to believe—to the Nile and wait for Pharaoh.[107] As Pharaoh approached, the staff reminded him about the truth weighing heavily on his heart.

Aaron said to Pharaoh: "This is what the Lord says: By this you will know that I am the Lord: With the staff that is in my hand I will strike the water of the Nile, and it will be changed into blood. The fish in the Nile will die, and the river will stink; the Egyptians will not be able to drink its water."[108]

Aaron stretched out the staff, and the waters of Egypt turned into blood.[109] Egypt's survival depended on the Nile River. The annual flooding fertilized the land, enabling the growth of crops that made their civilization thrive in a desert.[110] A ruined Nile meant the collapse of *maʿat*—the cosmic balance Pharaoh was sworn to uphold. God humiliated the idols the Egyptians believed sustained their civilization. He did more than tell Pharaoh, "I am Lord." He proved his power as Lord over creation by exposing the weakness of their idols to protect them.[111]

Pharaoh's priests dug around the river for clean water and proved they could turn water into blood too.[112] They imitated the disaster God sent but could not reverse it. Again, God strengthened Pharaoh's heart by giving him credible evidence that he is greater than the idols Egypt worships. But Pharaoh was not willing to admit his theology was wrong. With the stench from the Nile filling his nostrils, Pharaoh turned his back to God and went home.[113]

FROGS

God waited seven days for Pharaoh to repent. Then he said to Moses, "Go to Pharaoh and say to him, 'This is what the Lord says: Let my people go, so that they may worship me. If you refuse to let them go, I will send a plague of frogs on your whole country.'"[114]

Pharaoh refused to grant religious freedom. Frogs filled the land of Egypt. Again, Pharaoh's priests made the problem worse. They imitated the plague by producing more frogs but could not reverse it.

Frogs were sacred to the idol Heqet, the Egyptian goddess of fertility and childbirth. The plague directly challenged her power. Egypt usually welcomed the appearance of the frogs as a sign of renewal. Frogs swarming into their homes humiliated their idol, who could not control her own domain. Again, God exposed the inability of Egypt's idols to protect them.[115]

Pharaoh had absolute authority in political and religious matters. As the high priest of every temple, it was his duty to keep their idols happy. If he failed, the Egyptians believed the idols would withhold their blessings.[116] All of Pharaoh's idols, priests, wise men, armies, and wealth could not fix the disaster created by his pride, so he turned to the only one who could.

Pharaoh summoned Moses and Aaron. "Pray to the Lord to take the frogs away from me and my people, and I will let your people go to offer sacrifices to the Lord."[117]

Jesus said, "For by your words you will be acquitted, and by words you will be condemned."[118] The words Pharaoh spoke proved he knows Moses's God is Lord. He called him Lord twice when he promised them religious freedom if God removed the frogs.

ENEMY OF THE SINNER

God never commanded Pharaoh to worship him. He requested Pharaoh would let the Israelites worship the God of their ancestors. We are free to worship a lie. But we cross a line God will not tolerate when we forbid others to worship him and interfere in his efforts to keep a promise.

God is not against sinners. "For there is no difference between the Jew and the gentile, for all have sinned and fallen short of the glory of God."[119] God is against the enemy of the sinner. When a sinner knows the truth and interferes in the efforts of other sinners to worship a true and living God, he becomes the enemy of those sinners, and they become the objects of his wrath. But wrath is God's last option in dealing with his enemies. He first offers mercy by giving them time and credible reasons to obey him.[120] He has not become the enemy of Egypt's government yet.

DISCUSSION QUESTIONS

1. What does Pharaoh's strategy to discredit Moses teach about how oppressive systems maintain control?

2. What does the swallowing of the magicians' serpents symbolize about God's authority over Egypt's religious system?

3. What does Pharaoh's plea — "Pray to the **Lord**" — reveal about the shift happening inside him, even though he later resisted it?

4. How does Pharaoh's interference with Israel's worship move him closer to becoming God's enemy rather than simply a sinner in need of mercy?

5. What does God's patience with Pharaoh reveal about his character and his commitment to keeping his promises?

CHAPTER 11

THERE IS NO ONE LIKE HIM

Pharaoh knows Moses's God exists, and his power is greater than the idols he taught a nation to worship. He knows the God he is resisting is Lord. But his education has just begun. There is more that God wants Pharaoh to know.

Moses stood before Pharaoh as God's ambassador to offer deliverance from misery and said, "I leave to you the honor of setting the time for me to pray for you and your officials and your people that you and your houses may be rid of the frogs, except for those that remain in the Nile."

Pharaoh said, "Tomorrow!"

One word from Pharaoh not only extended his misery; he also extended the misery of everyone in Egypt. Why didn't he want the frogs removed today?

Moses replied, "It will be as you say, so that you may know there is no one like the Lord our God." [121]

When God offers deliverance, the time to accept is today. Tomorrow's deliverance will stink.[122] The following day, the frogs died. The Egyptians swept them out of their homes until heaps of dead frogs filled the streets and the stench spread everywhere. When Pharaoh saw that the plague of frogs had ended, he ignored the truth about God and reneged on his promise to give the Israelites religious freedom.

FINGER OF GOD

God responded to Pharaoh's stubbornness by sending the next plague without warning. He said to Moses, "Tell Aaron, 'Stretch out your staff and strike the dust of the ground,' and throughout the land of Egypt the dust will become lice." [123]

Lice covered the Egyptians and their animals. The Lector Priests, also covered with lice, tried to solve the problem by making more lice. They failed in their attempt to imitate God's power. When the priests said to Pharaoh, "this is the finger of God," they admitted the power behind Moses was greater than their magic.

Jesus later equated the "finger of God" as proof that the "kingdom of God has come upon you." [124] Egyptians believed their idols acted through *heka*, a power the priests channeled through spells and ritual objects. Their admission proved their spells, rituals, and idols were worthless. Their entire religious system could not stop the kingdom of God from controlling what happened in Egypt.[125]

PHARAOH'S HEART

God sought to heal Pharaoh's heart with evidence that worshipping their idols was vain. As Pharaoh's knowledge about God grew, his theology slowly unraveled. But his religious convictions were being challenged by a shepherd. The Egyptians viewed shepherds as an abomination.[126]

God resists the proud and gives grace to the humble by putting the truth in humble places. The indignity of being corrected by a common shepherd was too much to bear. Yet this shepherd, Moses, had credible evidence that his God is Lord. Even worse, Pharaoh's idols cannot help him prevail over the kingdom of God.

Pharaoh had too much power to lose if he gave Israel the freedom to worship a God he could not control. His pride made him an unreasonable fool. He did not hear because he did not want to hear.[127] The Apostle Paul called our bodies vessels that contain the truth about God. How we respond to the truth determines if we are a vessel to be honored or a worthless vessel.[128]

TOMORROW

Moses told Pharaoh, it will be as you say, so you may know there is no one like the Lord our God. When Pharaoh said "tomorrow," he set the standard God used to judge him. He wanted deliverance tomorrow, so God gave him what he wanted. From this point forward, God withheld his judgment against Pharaoh's rebellion until tomorrow.

God's use of Pharaoh's "tomorrow" was unique. When Pharaoh said tomorrow, his nation suffered one more day of misery. When God said tomorrow, he delayed their suffering one more day, giving them time to repent. Pharaoh and his priests are like the religious leaders Jesus called a brood of vipers. They could not bring forth good things because their hearts were evil.[129]

God's use of tomorrow proved he is good and there is no one like him. He could not bring forth an evil thing even when he repeated Pharaoh's evil "tomorrow." If Pharaoh had said he wanted relief next week, he would have been given a week to repent. If he had said next month, he would have been given a month to repent. Where sin abounds, grace abounds much more.[130]

LIES AND POWER

God sought to heal Pharaoh's heart by dispelling the darkness his theology created with credible evidence of his existence and power. Yet Pharaoh still refused to give the Israelites religious freedom. Why do we resist the truth and cling to the status quo when we know it's a lie? It happens today, just like it happened in Egypt. When a lie gives us power, it also gives us fear. Fear of losing power and its privileges is a house built on sand that will fall "with a great crash."[131]

DISCUSSION QUESTIONS

1. What lies—about God, yourself, or others—have given you a false sense of security?

2. Why was it especially humiliating for Pharaoh to be corrected by a shepherd, and what does this reveal about the danger of pride?

3. How does God's pattern of placing truth in humble vessels challenge our assumptions about authority and credibility?

4. How did God's decision to judge Pharaoh by his own words show both justice and mercy?

5. What did God's use of "tomorrow" reveal about his character?

CHAPTER 12

HE IS LORD IN EGYPT

God's mercy revealed the truth about Pharaoh. He is a liar. Pharaoh promised he would let Israel worship their God if God took the frogs away. When he was miserable, he was sincere. When the misery ended, so did his sincerity. Pharaoh's refusal to give the Israelites religious freedom is the reason the Nile was polluted with blood, the stench of decaying frogs permeated the air they breathed, and they were covered with biting lice. The kingdom of God had come upon them, not to destroy them but to open everyone's eyes to the truth. It did not matter how much credible evidence God gave to Pharaoh. He refused to love the truth that he might be saved.[132] Instead of destroying him, God continued Pharaoh's education.

FLIES

This time Aaron faded into the background, and Moses stepped into his calling. God told Moses to rise early and meet Pharaoh at the river with a message.

> "This is what the Lord says: Let my people go, so that they may worship me. If you do not let my people go, I will send swarms of flies[133] on you and your officials, on your people and into your houses. The houses of the Egyptians will be full of flies; even the ground will be covered with them. But on that day, I will deal differently with the land of Goshen, where my people live; no swarms of flies will be there, so that you will know that I, the Lord, am in this land. I will make a distinction between my people and your people. This sign will occur tomorrow."[134]

God spoke Pharaoh's tomorrow and brought forth good. Pharaoh had twenty-four hours to change his mind. Pharaoh's silence left God with no option but to do what he said. The following day, flies infested the land of Egypt, except for Goshen.

The plague of flies attacked the cosmic order their idols maintained. The harmony that kept creation stable, *ma'at* was crumbling. Egyptian theology suggested that their idols had been overpowered. The absence of flies in Goshen shook the foundation of their theology. Israel's God had drawn boundaries their idols could not cross.[135]

PHARAOH NEGOTIATES WITH GOD

Pharaoh's idols cannot control their own domains. The priests who served him were worthless. He had no recourse but to grant God's request lest Egypt descend into chaos. In his quest to remain relevant, he offered a compromise.

"Go, sacrifice to your God here in the land," he said to Moses and Aaron.[136]

The Egyptians practiced animal sacrifice, but the animals representing their idols were sacred. Sacrificing an animal that represented an idol carried the death penalty. Moses reminded Pharaoh of the death penalty if they sacrificed to their God in the land.

Pharaoh agreed. "I will let you go to offer sacrifices to the Lord your God in the wilderness, but you must not go very far. Now pray for me."[137]

FLAWED

Pharaoh had grown in the knowledge of God since he denied God's existence by calling Moses a liar. His attitude had softened. He might even be ripe for true repentance. But Moses proved to be as flawed as Pharaoh.

> "As soon as I leave you, I will pray to the Lord, and tomorrow the flies will leave Pharaoh and his officials and his people. Only let Pharaoh be sure that he does not act deceitfully again by not letting the people go to offer sacrifices to the Lord."[138]

God used tomorrow to extend mercy and delay the consequences of Pharaoh's rebellion. Why did Moses, servant of God, leave them in filth until tomorrow when he could have asked God to remove the flies today?

Pharaoh only hurt himself and his people with his evil tomorrow. Moses left Egypt in filth one more day while he enjoyed a pleasant evening in Goshen without one fly to annoy him. Was he angry because he did not like the way Pharaoh behaved? God never left them in misery one more day, like Pharaoh and Moses did.

PHARAOHS HEART

The next day, God removed the swarms of flies, proving his kingdom is superior to Pharaoh's, and he is Lord in Pharaoh's Egypt. Pharaoh buried the truth in a heart already heavy with truth and refused to keep his promise. Pharaoh's stubborn and unrepentant heart was building a case against him that would justify God when he judged him for the evil things he did.[139]

JUDGING OTHERS

Moses chided Pharaoh for being deceitful and demanded that he change his ways. Then he acted like Pharaoh by extending their misery one more day.[140] What would have happened if Moses had prayed to relieve Egypt's misery today instead of tomorrow? How many people have been driven away from God because we don't like the way they act and judge them worthy to suffer one more day?

DISCUSSION QUESTIONS

1. Pharaoh knew who God was yet refused to submit. Where in your own life do you recognize God's authority but still resist yielding control, and what would happen if you did?

2. God made a clear distinction between Egypt and Israel to show his care for his people. How have you seen God care for you in ways you didn't fully appreciate at the time?

3. Pharaoh tried to negotiate partial obedience with God. When are you tempted to offer God "almost obedience," and how does this chapter challenge you to give him your whole heart instead of selective surrender?

4. Moses faltered in his response to Pharaoh, reminding us that even God's servants can misstep. How does God's patience with Moses encourage you when you've mishandled a spiritual responsibility?

5. Pharaoh's hardened heart brought suffering to everyone under his authority. What does this teach you about the influence your choices have on your family, church, or community?

CHAPTER 13

COLLAPSE OF RELIGION

Pharaoh knows God exists, he is Lord, and there is no one like him. He knows God's kingdom has come and God is Lord in Pharaoh's Egypt. God proved he could keep his people safe when flies covered the Egyptians, but not one fly tormented his people. Yet Pharaoh ignored the truth and refused to give the Israelites religious freedom. God responded by giving Pharaoh another lesson about the God he was resisting.

A DISTINCTION

God sent Moses to Pharaoh with another message. "This is what the Lord, the God of the Israelites, says: "Let my people go, so that they may worship me. If you refuse to let them go and continue to hold them back, the hand of the Lord will bring a terrible plague on your livestock in the field—on your horses, donkeys, and camels, and on your cattle, sheep, and goats. But the Lord will make a distinction between the livestock of Israel and that of Egypt, so that no animal belonging to the Israelites will die... Tomorrow the Lord will do this in the land.'"[141]

Pharaoh had one more day to change his mind. Let the Israelites worship their God and none of Egypt's livestock would die. This is the first plague that was more than a major irritating nuisance. God's serpent humiliated Pharaoh's priests. During the plague of blood, the Egyptians dug around the river for water to drink. The frogs made the land stink. The lice made them itch, and the flies made everything filthy.

DEATH

The next plague targeted the rich and powerful. Only the wealthy owned livestock and ate meat. The average Egyptian was a vegetarian who ate meat on special occasions. The death of Egypt's livestock had the greatest effect on the wealthy. It foreshadowed the wages of sin Egypt would receive if they continued to deny the Israelites freedom to worship their God.[142]

The following day, the livestock in Egypt died. Pharaoh sent a delegation to Goshen to verify if the Israelites' livestock were affected. They returned to Pharaoh with unwelcome news. None of the Israelites' livestock died. How much credible evidence of God's power did Pharaoh need? Did Pharaoh think God could kill animals but not the Egyptians?

BOILS

Again, Pharaoh ignored the truth. Again, God responded with mercy. He gave Pharaoh one more reason to believe that their religion and its idols were worthless. God instructed Moses to scatter ashes toward the heavens in the sight of Pharaoh. The ashes became fine dust that produced festering boils on the Egyptians.

The Egyptians believed evil spirits entered their bodies to create lesions as a divine punishment for sin.[143] They wore amulets to keep evil spirits away. But their remedies failed. The boils covering the priests marked them as sinners and disqualified them from service in their temples. With no one to lead worship, the temples closed.[144]

The Egyptians built a great house on sand. The religion they relied on to protect them and justify Pharaoh's throne shattered in a storm of truth. The wind of evil doctrine they sowed produced a whirlwind of disaster when their own theology screamed, "You are sinners."[145]

PHARAOH'S HEART

God sought to heal Pharaoh's heart with an abundance of reasons to believe and confirmed those reasons with verifiable evidence. Each plague added to the weight of truth. God did not come to Egypt to condemn Pharaoh. Pharaoh condemned himself when he repeatedly ignored the truth. No matter how much credible evidence God gave him to believe, he refused to give the Israelites religious freedom.

Egyptians believed chaos would ensue if Pharaoh failed to appease their idols.[146] The collapse of their religion and the authority it gave Pharaoh to rule should have brought them to repentance. Egyptian theology shouted they are on a path to chaos. Yet the government continued to support a mere man playing god.

DISCUSSION QUESTIONS

1. God made a clear distinction between Egypt and Israel, protecting his people while judging Pharaoh's rebellion. How does God's ability to make distinctions encourage you when you feel surrounded by circumstances you cannot control?

2. Pharaoh repeatedly ignored credible evidence of God's power and mercy.

Where in your own life has God given you repeated truth, or warnings to change, and what keeps you from responding fully?

3. The collapse of Egypt's religion exposed the emptiness of their idols and the false security they offered. What modern "religious systems," or sources of security do people rely on today, and how can you guard your heart from trusting something that cannot save or sustain you?

4. God's judgments were not designed to destroy Pharaoh but to heal his heart by confronting lies with truth. How has God used difficult experiences in your life to reveal truth so he could draw you closer to him?

5. Pharaoh feared chaos if he obeyed God, yet the real chaos came from resisting him.

In what area of your life are you tempted to hold on to control, and how might surrendering that area to God bring peace rather than chaos?

CHAPTER 14

NO ONE LIKE HIM ON EARTH

Pharaoh can no longer claim, "I do not know the Lord." He knows God exists, that he is Lord, and there is no one like him. He knows God's kingdom has come to Egypt. Pharaoh is no longer in control, because Moses's God is Lord in Egypt. Pharaoh knows his priests cannot undo what God has done. He knows God is greater than the idols he taught a nation to worship. But there is more Pharaoh needs to know.

WARNING

God told Moses to rise early in the morning and bring Pharaoh another message. "This is what the Lord God of the Israelites, says: Let my people go, so that they may worship me, or this time I will send the full force of my plagues against you and against your officials and your people, so that you may know that there is no one like me in all the earth. For by now I could have stretched out my hand and struck you and your people with a plague that would have wiped you off the earth. But I have raised you up for this very purpose, that I might show you my power and that my name might be proclaimed in all the earth. You still set yourself against my people and will not let them go. Therefore, at this time tomorrow I will send the worst hailstorm that has ever fallen on Egypt, from the day it was founded till now. Give an order now to bring your livestock and everything you have in the field to a place of shelter, because the hail will fall on every person and animal that has not been brought in and is still out in the field, and they will die."[147]

God was in Egypt fighting for the right of his people to worship him. He never demanded Pharaoh to worship him. He could have sent a pestilence to kill Pharaoh and his people the first time he refused to obey. Killing them would have been easy. But God was not their enemy. He proved his love for the Egyptians when he warned them about the coming disaster and told them how to escape death. God is not willing that any should perish, even hard-hearted Pharaoh and the foolish people who continue to support him as their nation descends into chaos.

Some of Pharaoh's servants heeded God's warning. They sent their servants and livestock to a safe place.[148] Then God said to Moses, "Stretch out your hand toward heaven, that there may be hail in all the land of Egypt—on man, on beast, and on every herb of the field, throughout the land of Egypt."[149]

Thunder boomed, lightning flashed, creating fireballs that darted along the ground as a deluge of hail covered the land. The hail destroyed the herbs of the field. People and animals left in the field died. Hail did not fall in Goshen, where the Israelites lived.

The Egyptians would have recognized the storm as a battle among gods. They believed lightning, thunder, and destructive weather indicated a divine being asserting his supremacy. The intensity of the storm suggested a foreign deity had overridden the authority of their idols. This new God dismantled their theology by proving his power over the domains protected by their idols.[150]

I HAVE SINNED

From the safety of his palace, Pharaoh watched his servants running to escape death. One after another struck down in a storm of hail. Their blood soaked the ground. Pharaoh knows he could have prevented this tragedy. One command from his lips and all of Egypt would have stayed home that day. Instead, the blood of the innocent cried out against him as the wealth of Egypt vanished in a rain of hail and fire.

Pharaoh can argue with Moses. He can argue with his priests and wise men. Pharaoh can even argue with God. But he cannot argue with the voice of his own actions. He summoned Moses and Aaron to his throne room. The guilt of his selfishness burst through the wall of his resistance, allowing the heavy weight of truth to flow from his mouth. "This time I have sinned; the Lord is in the right, and I and my people are in the wrong."[151]

This time? Half of Pharaoh's statement is true. The Lord is right. Egypt is wrong. But this was not the first time Pharaoh and his people sinned.

Pharaoh asked Moses to intercede to the only God who could help him and his people. "Pray to the Lord, for we have had enough thunder and hail. I will let you go; you don't have to stay any longer." [152]

Moses agreed to pray as soon as he exited the city limits. They would not have to wait until tomorrow for relief. The hail would stop today, so Pharaoh and everyone throughout time could know there is no one like Israel's God in all the earth. He alone can stop the storms in our lives we create with disobedience.

Then Moses declared, "I know that you and your officials still do not fear the Lord God." [153]

Moses finally learned what God had known from the beginning. People who know the truth and reject it will never fear God and change their ways. God never needed Pharaoh's permission for the Israelites to leave Egypt. But he wanted more than just the Israelites and Egyptians to know him. God wanted everyone to the ends of the earth throughout time to know him. God educated Pharaoh to educate us.

IN THE CALM

God had strengthened Pharaoh's heart with one more reason to believe.[154] But in the calm that followed Moses's intercession, Pharaoh and his people hardened their hearts. The officials, who continued to serve a man playing God knowing he was doing wrong, became like their master.[155] Pharaoh's power came not from God, but from the people who served him.

God gave Egypt one more reason to believe and obey him. Pharaoh admitted that he and his people were sinners.

They know God is righteous. Even though Pharaoh said for the third time that he would let Israel worship their God, Moses knew his character had not changed. As soon as the misery left, so did his desire to let the Israelites worship their God. It's not enough to know the truth and admit we are sinners. We must change our ways.

NOW WE KNOW

Now Pharaoh knows there is no one like God in all the earth. His power is his mercy that calms the storm in our lives when we admit the truth and ask for help. Pharaoh had come a long way since he declared he did not know God and would not let the Israelites worship him.

Throughout history, many have acknowledged they are sinners, yet they refuse to obey God because they don't want to. We are free to live as we choose. We are not free from the consequences of our choices.

God patiently endures sinful people, so we can learn what God and now Moses knows. If we don't know the truth about God, he might lose us too. Sometimes the religious people we love lead us astray. Most are good people, zealous for God, who were taught false doctrine. The problem is clinging to false doctrine when faced with the truth. We will not accept God's judgment against them until we learn what Moses learned.

DISCUSSION QUESTIONS

1. God warned Pharaoh and even told the Egyptians how to escape the coming judgment. What does this reveal about God's heart toward people who oppose him, and how does that challenge the way you treat those who resist truth?

2. Some of Pharaoh's servants believed God's warning and acted, while others ignored it. When God gives you a warning, what helps you respond with obedience instead of delay?

3. Pharaoh confessed, "This time I have sinned," yet he refused to change. Where in your life are you tempted to acknowledge sin without actually turning from it, and what step of obedience would demonstrate real repentance?

4. The storm stopped the moment Moses prayed, showing that God alone can calm the chaos we create. What "storms" in your life are the result of your own choices, and how might turning to God in humility bring peace?

5. Pharaoh knew the truth, but hardened his heart once the crisis passed. How can you guard yourself from returning to old patterns once God brings relief, and what spiritual practice could help you remain faithful in the calm as well as the storm?

CHAPTER 15

THAT ISRAEL MAY KNOW

A turning point had come in God's dealings with Pharaoh. When we know the truth and reject it, the only option left is "to reserve the unjust unto the day of judgment to be punished."[156]

Knowing Pharaoh would never change, God continued to give him credible, verifiable reasons to fear him to the very end, with one exception. God told Moses, "I have hardened (*kabad*) Pharaoh's heart and the hearts of his officials."[157] God made their hearts heavy with the truth they did not want to believe. Then he instructed Moses to tell his children and grandchildren how God dealt with the Egyptians, so future generations would remember their God is Lord.

LOCUST

God sent Moses and Aaron to Pharaoh with a message: "How long will you refuse to humble yourself before me?

Let my people go, so that they may worship me. If you refuse to let them go, I will bring locusts into your country tomorrow. They will cover the face of the ground so that it cannot be seen. They will devour what little you have left after the hail, including every tree that is growing in your fields. They will fill your houses and those of all your officials and all the Egyptians—something neither your parents nor your ancestors have ever seen from the day they settled in this land till now."[158]

LET THE MEN GO

Knowing Pharaoh would never change his ways, Moses did not wait for a reply. After he left, Pharaoh's officials reconsidered. "How long will this man be a snare to us? Let the people go, so that they may worship the Lord their God. Do you not yet realize that Egypt is ruined?"[159]

Pharaoh heeded the counsel of his officials. He summoned Moses and Aaron for another meeting. "Go, worship the Lord your God,...But tell me who will be going."[160]

Moses said, "Everyone including our flocks and herds."[161]

Pharaoh replied, "No! Have only the men go, and worship the Lord, since that's what you have been asking for."[162] The Easy-to-Read Version of the Bible says, "That is what you asked for in the beginning."

This conversation left Moses naked for all to see and learn. Until this meeting, Moses had only asked Pharaoh to let the men go into the wilderness to worship God. But God wanted everyone to worship him. Somewhere between the first meeting with Pharaoh and this one, God corrected Moses.

Pharaoh did not like this unexpected change. To maintain some control and keep his officials happy, Pharaoh granted Moses's original request for the men to travel three days into the wilderness and worship God. Then he cast them out of his throne room.

I SENT MIRIAM TOO

Many years after the Exodus, God said to Israel through the prophet Micah, "I brought you up out of Egypt and redeemed you from the land of slavery. I sent Moses to lead you, also Aaron and Miriam."[163] God sent three people to lead the nation. Yet Miriam is noticeably absent from the negotiations with Pharaoh.

In the beginning of their negotiations, Moses acted like an Egyptian when he denied his sister her place in leadership and all women the opportunity to accompany them into the wilderness to worship God. If God had not intervened, Moses would have left the women in Egypt.

Throughout history, those who serve God have possessed partial knowledge about him and his intentions. Their culture sometimes influenced their beliefs about God. The concept that only men can be leaders, prevalent in much of Christianity today, has its roots in the Egyptian religion.[164] This concept of leadership would have been comfortable to both Moses, raised by Pharaoh's daughter, and Aaron influenced by Egyptian culture. But God's ways are not the ways of Egypt. Miriam had a valid ministry to fulfill as a leader of the nation. If God had let them leave without the women, they would have been a body handicapped by a missing part.[165]

I HAVE SINNED AGAIN

God instructed Moses to stretch out his staff over Egypt. A strong east wind blew all day and night. That morning, a vast army of locusts settled in Egypt. Egyptians would have viewed the plague of locusts as a catastrophic event. Locusts advanced across Egypt like dark clouds blotting out the sun's rays. Their idol's inability to protect them shook their theology to its core. A superior divine authority was in the land, and Pharaoh was powerless before him.[166]

The locust proceeded to devour everything edible that had survived the previous plagues. Alarmed by the famine that would follow, Pharaoh called for Moses and Aaron to return with haste. "I have sinned against the Lord your God and against you. Now forgive my sin once more and pray to the Lord your God to take this deadly plague away from me."

The first time Pharaoh repented, he acknowledged his sin against God. This time he included his sin against the Israelites for denying them freedom of religion. Moses left the throne room and prayed God would end the plague of locusts. As Pharaoh anxiously awaited God's reply, the strong east wind became a strong west wind that blew the locusts into the Nile.

Again, God gave Pharaoh another reason to believe and obey him. The prophet Jeremiah told us why. "Because of the Lord's great love we are not consumed, for his compassions never fail. They are new every morning."[167] Egypt did not have to spend one more day with the locusts. Where sin abounded, grace did much more abound.[168] God's kindness leads us to repentance, but it does not guarantee our repentance is sincere.[169] Pharaoh showed contempt for God's kindness, restraint, and patience. After admitting twice that he had sinned, he still refused to give Israel religious freedom.

God has mercy on whom he will have mercy. His mercy gives us the strength to believe he is good. When God gives us reasons to believe, it can harden us into a stubborn Abraham, who against all hope believed God would do what he promised,[170] or harden us into a foolish Pharaoh. It is our choice.

DISCUSSION QUESTIONS

1. How does God's persistence in giving Pharaoh "credible, verifiable reasons to believe" reveal his character, and where in your own life has God continued to show you truth you resisted or ignored?

2. God corrected Moses's limited understanding of leadership by insisting that women be included in worship and ministry. What does this teach us about God's commitment to restoring what culture distorts, and where might God be correcting your assumptions today?

3. Pharaoh confessed, "I have sinned," yet refused to obey. What does this teach us about the difference between admitting wrong and truly repenting, and how can you guard your heart from Pharaoh like patterns of temporary remorse?

4. God's mercy removed the locusts "so Egypt did not have to spend one more day with them." How does this display God's compassion even toward those who oppose him, and how might remembering God's compassion change the way you treat difficult people?

5. The chapter ends by showing that God's mercy can harden a person into a stubborn Abraham (who believes) or a stubborn Pharaoh (who resists). What practices help you respond to God's mercy with faith rather than resistance?

CHAPTER 16

AN UNACCEPTABLE OFFER

Pharaoh knows the truth. He knows God exists and there is no one like him. He knows God's kingdom is in Egypt. Pharaoh knows God is not only Lord in Egypt; there is no one like him in all the earth. But the education of Pharaoh is not over.

DARKNESS

Jesus said, "Light has come into the world, but people loved darkness instead of light because their deeds were evil."[171] Pharaoh and his followers loved darkness, so God gave them what they loved. He told Moses to stretch out his hand toward heaven, so darkness would cover Egypt, except in the land of Goshen where the Israelites lived. A heavy darkness made it difficult for the Egyptians to move about freely. Pharaoh let his nation suffer for three days before he changed his mind.

DEATH

He summoned Moses and made another offer. "Go, worship the Lord. Even your women and children may go with you; only leave your flocks and herds behind."[172]

"You must allow us to have sacrifices and burnt offerings to present to the Lord our God. Our livestock too must go with us; not a hoof is to be left behind," said Moses.

Pharaoh became angry with God's messenger. "Get out of my sight! Make sure you do not appear before me again! The day you see my face, you will die."[173]

"Just as you say," Moses replied. "I will never appear before you again...This is what the Lord says: 'About midnight I will go throughout Egypt. Every firstborn son in Egypt will die, from the firstborn son of Pharaoh, who sits on the throne, to the firstborn son of the female slave, who is at her handmill, and all the firstborn of the cattle as well. There will be loud wailing throughout Egypt—worse than there has ever been or ever will be again. But among the Israelites not a dog will bark at any person or animal.'"[174]

Before Moses left, "hot with anger," he warned Pharaoh that his officials would override him to give the Israelites religious freedom if he did not let them leave with their livestock.[175]

God had already proved to Pharaoh that he did not desire to kill anyone. When he sent the plague of hail that could kill the Egyptians, he told Pharaoh how to keep everyone and their flocks alive.

But Pharaoh refused to receive the love of the truth that he might be saved.[176] In a moment of anger, he sealed his fate. When people know the truth and reject it, God sends a powerful delusion to condemn all who delight in wickedness.[177] He will destroy the wicked government of Egypt, but first he left a way to save the nation.

SAVING EGYPT

God told Abraham his descendants would leave the country that oppressed them with many possessions.[178] He repeated that promise to Moses at the burning bush when he said, "And I will make the Egyptians favorably disposed toward this people, so that when you leave, you will not go empty-handed. Every woman is to ask her neighbor and any woman living in her house for articles of silver and gold and for clothing, which you will put on your sons and daughters, and so you will plunder the Egyptians."[179]

The English word plunder, used as a noun, means the violent and dishonest acquisition of property. When used as a verb, it means to steal goods in times of war or civil disorder. The Hebrew word translated as plunder can be used in a good sense, meaning to deliver, or in a bad sense, meaning to spoil.

The English meaning of plunder was never God's intent. The Israelites never started a war or created civil disorder. They waited while their God fought the battle for their religious freedom. God gave his people favor with the Egyptians, so he could bless Egypt, whose corrupt government had destroyed the nation.

The law God later gave to Moses explains why he made the Egyptians willing to give the Israelites their wealth. In the covenant of Law, when the Israelites release a servant, they must not send the servant away empty-handed. They must supply him or her with the things he or she needs and not consider it a hardship. God will compensate the loss by blessing them in everything they do.[180] God guaranteed Egypt sent the Israelites away supplied with the things they needed, so he could save Egypt by blessing the Egyptians in everything they did. Egypt exists to this day.

God does not plunder people. Those who plunder others don't ask. They take advantage of them when they are too weak to defend themselves. God told his people to ask. From the very beginning of God's dealings with Israel and Egypt, he intended to bless both nations.

BLIND LEADING THE BLIND

For no other reason than Pharaoh could not dictate how the Israelites would worship, he cut off the only way to get relief from the darkness. We might think it's not fair to the people Pharaoh ruled. But they were just as hard-hearted and foolish as Pharaoh. The people cast Israel's newborn baby boys into the Nile to drown.[181] The professional clergy told Pharaoh, "This is the finger of God." His officials told him Egypt was destroyed. They knew Pharaoh's disobedience created their suffering. So why were they enabling a megalomaniac?[182]

If they loved their nation more than the power and privilege Pharaoh gave them, they would have stopped him from resisting Israel's God, who proved he was more powerful than Pharaoh and all the idols of Egypt.

When we continue to support a wicked man, knowing he is doing wrong, we are just as guilty as he is.[183] Why shouldn't we suffer what our leader suffers, when we are his enablers? Let them alone, Jesus said, "They are blind leaders of the blind. And if the blind lead the blind, both will fall into a ditch."[184]

DISCUSSION QUESTIONS

1. What does God's refusal to accept Pharaoh's partial obedience reveal about his character, and how does that challenge the areas in your life where you negotiate with God instead of surrendering fully?

2. Pharaoh offered a compromise that looked spiritual but still kept control. In what ways can religious activity become a substitute for true obedience in your own walk with God?

3. How does this chapter show that God defines the terms of worship, and what practical steps can you take to align your worship with God's standards rather than your preferences?

4. Pharaoh's offer required Israel to stay close enough to Egypt to remain under his influence. What influences in your life try to keep you spiritually "near Egypt," and how is God calling you to step farther into freedom?

5. God's response to Pharaoh demonstrates that partial obedience is still disobedience. Where is God inviting you to move from partial obedience to wholehearted obedience?

CHAPTER 17

MIDNIGHT

In the death of the firstborn sons, God made no difference between the Egyptians and the Israelites. He made a way of escape for both when he told Moses how to keep the firstborn safe. On the fourteenth day of that month, every family must slaughter a lamb at twilight and put the lamb's blood on the sides and tops of the doorframes of their houses.

God said, "The blood will be a sign for you on the houses where you are, and when I see the blood, I will pass over you. No destructive plague will touch you when I strike Egypt."[185]

It did not matter who was in the house. The blood on the door stopped death, making the house a haven for the firstborn. Had the Egyptian firstborn put aside their religious bias against Israel and stayed overnight with an Israelite family, they also would have been saved from death.[186]

AFTER MIDNIGHT

Pharaoh denied Moses's request for religious freedom because he did not know God. He no longer had that excuse. Who has received more credible evidence of God's existence and power than Pharaoh? He proved he would rather sit in darkness than let the Israelites worship their God by ending the negotiations with a threat to kill Moses. Did Pharaoh think God would keep his word nine times but not ten?

After the midnight hour, Pharaoh's officials awoke him. Every family in Egypt was wailing in grief over losing a loved one. Pharaoh remembered God's warning that he would kill Egypt's firstborn sons and animals if Pharaoh refused to let Israel worship him. He ran to the room of his firstborn son to learn God kept his word.

Pharaoh summoned Moses and Aaron to concede defeat. "Up! Leave my people, you and the Israelites! Go, worship the Lord as you have requested. Take your flocks and herds, as you have said, and go. And also bless me."[187]

Pharaoh finally humbled himself by submitting to God's request. But he only did it because his officials thought everyone would die. He knew they would remove him from power before they let that happen.[188] Then he had the audacity to ask for a blessing, but it's too late.

"He who is often rebuked, and hardens his neck, will suddenly be destroyed, and that without remedy."[189] We reap what we sow. If we know the truth about God yet resist him to satisfy our own desires, we will reap destruction.[190]

God is merciful to the unthankful and the ungrateful. But mercy only delays judgment, giving us time to repent. "God cannot be mocked."[191] If his lovingkindness and mercy cannot persuade us to change our ways, we will reap what we have sown.

GOD'S PLAN

God told Moses to camp by the sea, so Pharaoh would think they were lost. Trapped by the sea, they could not escape. Even though God knows it won't do any good, he strengthened Pharaoh's heart with another reason to believe.

When messengers reported the Israelites had fled, his officials said, "What have we done? We have let the Israelites go and have lost their services!"[192]

The same officials who told Pharaoh to let Israel worship their God, became like their leader. Those same officials subsequently persuaded Pharaoh, who encouraged his officials to oppose divine authority, to resume his resistance, ultimately leading to their death. With their support, Pharaoh called for his chariot and ordered the captains of six hundred choice chariots, his horsemen, and his infantry to report for duty.[193]

GOD'S PRESENCE

When the Israelites left Egypt, an angel of God traveled with them, and God appeared among them in a "pillar of cloud to guide them on their way by day, and by night a pillar of fire to give them light..."[194] As they were setting up camp by the Red Sea, the Israelites saw the vast army of Egypt approaching.

They cried out to God for help and then got mad at Moses. "Was it because there were no graves in Egypt that you brought us to the desert to die? What have you done to us by bringing us out of Egypt? Didn't we say to you in Egypt, 'Leave us alone; let us serve the Egyptians?' It would have been better for us to serve the Egyptians than to die in the desert!"[195]

Moses assured the Israelites that this would be the last time they saw the Egyptians. They needed to be quiet while God fought for them. Then Moses, who knew why God told them to camp by the sea and that Pharaoh would not be successful, cried out to the Lord for help.

The only ones who needed help were the Egyptians. God gave the government of Egypt one last opportunity to repent and obey him by strengthening their hearts with credible evidence of his existence and power. God and his angel moved to the rear of the camp.[196] He had one last item on his agenda: "Those who hate him he will repay to their face by destruction; he will not be slow to repay to their face those who hate him."[197]

Pharaoh thought he would force the Israelites back to Egypt. Instead, he came face to face with God to receive the reward for his evil deeds. God gave his enemies darkness to keep them separated from his people. He gave his people light while he prepared a way of escape. Then God commanded Moses to stretch his staff over the sea. All night a strong east wind blew, dividing the water into two walls and drying the ground between the walls of water.[198]

Pharaoh and his officials had all night to consider the sanity of their actions. They thought they needed slaves to prosper as a nation, but they did not. God had already made a way to bless their nation when he gave Israel favor with the Egyptians, and they willingly gave Israel their gold, silver, and clothing. The Egyptians could have returned home and prospered. Instead, they pursued Israel into the way of escape God had created for his people.

God knocked the wheels off the Egyptians' chariots, slowing their pursuit until Israel reached safety on the opposite shore. Israel heard the Egyptians screaming confirmation that God fights the battles of his people. "Let's get away from the Israelites!" the Egyptians cried. "The Lord is fighting for them against Egypt."[199] God commanded Moses to raise his staff over the sea again, and the walls of water collapsed on the Egyptians. The way of escape for Isreal became a grave for their oppressors.

FINAL EXAM

Pharaoh made an F for fatality on his final exam, and so did his followers. The people who served Pharaoh became like him. They chose darkness and followed a blind man to their death. The education of Pharaoh ended in a watery grave, or did it just begin? God educated Pharaoh to educate us![200]

DISCUSSION QUESTIONS

1. Are you in a "midnight moment" — a place where everything feels dark and delayed — and how does this chapter challenge you to respond differently than fear or frustration would suggest?

2. The chapter highlights God working in hidden or unexpected ways. What is one situation in your life right now where you need to trust that God is active even when you cannot see progress?

3. Midnight often exposes what we truly believe. What recent situation revealed your instinctive response — faith, worry, self reliance, or something else — and what does that show you about where God is inviting growth?

4. God's timing is purposeful, not accidental. How might your perspective shift if you viewed your current problem as preparation for deliverance?

5. When God moves at "midnight," His people must be ready. What practical step can you take this week to prepare your heart to worship God in your wilderness?

CHAPTER 18

THE STRUGGLE CONTINUES

The Israelites experienced the fulfillment of an ancient promise when they walked on dry land to freedom. "Let's get away from the Israelites! The LORD is fighting for them against Egypt"[201] echoed in their thoughts as they watched the walls of water collapse on their oppressors.[202]

But only a remnant of the Israelites remained faithful to worship God alone. Most had complained all the way to Mt. Sinai, where they entered into a covenant with God and promised, "We will do everything the Lord has said; we will obey."[203]

A mere forty days later, they asked Aaron to make them an idol to lead them. He made a gold calf, and they presented the calf to the nation. "This is your god, O Israel, who brought you up from the land of Egypt."[204] Aaron built an altar before the calf and announced, "Tomorrow there will be a festival before the Lord."

God told Moses that the people had already broken their covenant with him. Before Moses returned to the camp, he prayed God would not be angry and would forgive them. Moses came down the mountain to see people dancing and singing before a golden calf. It made him so angry that he broke the tablets God himself had written the covenant on.

They continued their journey to the Promised Land, but the people refused to enter. They claimed they would be better off if they had died in Egypt or in the wilderness. God responded by teaching them what it means to know his breach of promise.[205] He gave them an option they preferred. Death in the wilderness. But God did not abandon the nation. He sustained them for forty years in the wilderness with manna, the food of angels, and did not let their clothes wear out.[206]

The children bore the consequences of their fathers' sin as they waited for the rebellious generation to die.[207] Then God split the Jordan River and brought the children of rebels into Canaan. Joshua conquered thirty-one kings and distributed their land among the tribes. But the children who possessed the land failed to learn from their fathers' failure. Their hearts clung to Egypt's idols, and they added new idols from the surrounding nations to their collection of false gods.[208]

Then Israel rejected God's love for the rule of a human king.[209] God gave them Saul, a disobedient king, and then David, a righteous king. Solomon, the son of King David, pleased God when he asked for wisdom to judge righteously. He made Solomon the wisest man who ever lived.[210] But wisdom without love availed nothing.

Solomon betrayed God and his nation when he openly worshiped the idols his many wives loved.

THE LIE

The lie Aaron taught God's people survived hundreds of years and flourished again when God split the nation. He gave ten tribes to Jeroboam, who became king of Israel. He left the tribes of Judah and Benjamin to King David's children.

Motivated by fear the people would abandon him if they worshiped at the temple in Jerusalem, Jeroboam made two gold calves and repeated Aaron's lie.[211] The worship of the golden calves endured for generations because the people believed they were worshiping the God who had delivered them from Egypt.

THE SOURCE

After God scattered Israel and Judah to live in foreign nations for breaking their covenant with him, he showed Ezekiel the source of their problems in a vision. He brought Ezekiel to the Temple in Jerusalem and pointed to a large idol at the entrance of the north gate. "Son of dust, do you see what they are doing? Do you see what great sins the people of Israel are doing here, to push me from my Temple? But come I will show you greater sins than these!" [212]

He brought Ezekiel to the door of the Temple courtyard, where he commanded him to dig his way into the temple through a hole in the wall. Ezekiel entered a hidden room where he saw the elders of Israel worshiping images of snakes and hideous creatures that covered the walls.[213]

Then God said, “Son of dust, have you seen what the elders of Israel are doing in their minds?”

The elders were worshiping snakes and hideous creatures because they thought, “the Lord does not see us; the Lord has forsaken the land.”[214] Our beliefs govern our actions. Believing God had forsaken them, the elders forsook God and openly worshipped idols. The nation followed their example except for a remnant who remained faithful to God.

THE KEY

Religious leaders teaching people a false image of God is not unique to the ancient Israelites. Jesus warned his disciples that they would face abuse in the synagogues because they spoke the truth he had taught them. Paul warned the saints at Ephesus about cruel and greedy religious leaders, full of selfish ambition, who would distort the truth about God to attract a following.[215]

Today, there are hundreds of Christian denominations in the United States and thousands globally. Each has distinctive interpretations of scripture that differ from other denominations. The various interpretations and partial knowledge we possess about God make finding an accurate image of God difficult, but not impossible.

Jesus’s greatest opponents were religious leaders, but his ministry also produced many priests “obedient to the faith.”[216] He told his disciples to listen to their rabbis because they teach the law of Moses. Then he pointed to the rabbis’ failures of character and warned his followers not to behave like them.[217]

Jesus also gave his disciples the key to finding an accurate image of God.

> "But do not be called Rabbi (Teacher); for One is your Teacher, and you are all [equally] brothers. Do not call anyone on earth [who guides you spiritually] your father; for One is your Father, He who is in heaven. Do not let yourselves be called leaders or teachers; for One is your Leader (Teacher), the Christ. But the greatest among you will be your servant."—Matthew 23:8-11 Amplified Bible

God confirmed Jesus's statement about leaders and teachers during Jesus's transfiguration in the presence of Peter, James, and John. Moses and Elijah appeared to speak with Jesus. Peter interrupted Jesus's conversation with an offer to build each of them a tabernacle. God did not approve. He pointed the disciples to Jesus when he said, "This is my son, whom I love; with him I am well pleased. Listen to him."[218]

When Jesus returned to heaven, it appeared communicating with him would be nonexistent. But he assured his grieving disciples it was better for him to leave them. If he left, he would send the Spirit of truth to be with us forever.[219]

The Spirit of truth arrived on the Day of Pentecost to dwell in the believer, giving us equal access to God.[220] Jesus, and later the Apostle John, assured us we have an incorruptible teacher in the Holy Spirit.[221]

> "As for you, the anointing [the special gift, the preparation] which you received from Him remains [permanently] in you, and you have no need for anyone to teach you. But just as His anointing teaches you

> [giving you insight through the presence of the Holy Spirit] about all things, and is true and is not a lie, and just as His anointing has taught you, you must remain in Him [being rooted in Him, knit to Him]."— 1 John 2:27 AMP

The Holy Spirit came to earth bearing the good and perfect gifts we need to understand the word of God. The Spirit distributes those gifts to each believer according to God's will for the common good. While one may have a gift for teaching, that person is not the teacher. He or she is a servant whom the Holy Spirit uses to teach others.

THE GIFT

Paul wrote to the Christians in Rome, "Do not conform to the pattern of this world..."[222] Judaism formed Saul's perception of God before he became the Apostle Paul. Idol worship influenced the gentile Christian's thoughts about God. We cannot mix the way the world worships with Christianity and find an accurate image of God. We must renew our minds about God by separating human thoughts from God's thoughts and intentions for us.

Renewing our minds is more than an acquisition of knowledge about God. Human teachers can give us information but lack the ability to impart understanding. The disciples saw God in the person of Jesus. They heard him speak and asked him questions. Yet Jesus often felt frustrated because his disciples lacked understanding.[223]

Jesus spoke about a day when we will worship God in Spirit and in truth. Paul told us that God gave us his Spirit because no one knows God's thoughts except the Spirit of God. God gave us the Spirit of truth to reveal his thoughts so we can understand what he has freely given to us.[224] After Jesus's resurrection, he appeared to his disciples and "opened their minds so they could understand the scripture."[225] In Jesus's absence, the Holy Spirit imparts insight about God that enables us to discern God's good, pleasing, and perfect will.[226]

We are subject to being blown about by every new wind of doctrine that distorts the image of God until we become spiritually mature.[227] The Galatian church wrestled with this problem. Christian Jews came to Galatia preaching a different gospel that required Gentiles to obey the law God gave to Moses to be saved. Many Galatians were deserting Jesus's gift of grace to earn their salvation by obeying laws.

The Apostle Paul considered the Galatian church the children he gave birth to by preaching the gospel of salvation by faith.[228] He wrote to the Galatians, "I did not receive it from any man, nor was I taught it; rather, I received it by revelation from Jesus Christ."[229] Paul compared himself to a woman suffering labor pains again until a true image of Christ was "completely and permanently"[230] formed within them.

Maintaining an accurate image of God is a spiritual battle that must be fought with spiritual weapons. Therefore, God sent the Holy Spirit with gifts to help us fight the spiritual battle for truth.[231] God's good and perfect gifts enable us to tear down proud thoughts that exalt themselves against the knowledge of God.[232] These proud thoughts distort the image of God in our minds into the gold calves we worship, believing we are worshiping the God who delivered us, when we are only worshiping a lie about God.[233]

The important task of acquiring an accurate image of God to worship is the responsibility of the individual believer.[234] Without the Holy Spirit's help, all we have is knowledge we don't fully understand. Jesus assured us if we ask for the Holy Spirit, he will give us his Spirit. If we seek him, we will find him. If we knock, the door will open for his Spirit to create an accurate image of God to worship.[235]

WAITING

The author of Hebrews confirmed Israel never received the fulfillment of God's promises to Abraham.[236] While they were in the wilderness, God swore an oath that the people who tested him ten times would never enter his rest.[237] Before Moses died, God gave him a song to teach Israel, so they would remember that their nation would fail.

Joshua led them into the Promised Land, but he did not give them the rest an incorruptible government gives us. Israel continued to worship idols, and lusted for a human king, when God was already their king. God told them a human king would not be good, but they insisted. He gave them what they wanted.

Saul, their first king, was more concerned about losing power than obeying God. David, the second king, shamed the nation when he committed adultery with Bathsheba and then arranged the murder of her husband. Solomon, the third king, publicly worshiped idols to please his many wives. It did not take long for the wisest man on earth to lead his nation into open rebellion.[238] Israel never had the incorruptible government Abraham left Ur of the Chaldees to find.[239] Only Jesus can give us rest from corruption. Until he returns, we wait.

While we wait, we have a choice to make. When God revealed himself to Pharaoh with irrefutable evidence of his existence and power, Pharaoh refused to change his mind about the religious practices he embraced, and he lost everything. Now that you know what God taught Pharaoh, it's time for you to choose.

> "If you declare with your mouth, "Jesus is Lord," and believe in your heart that God raised him from the dead, you will be saved. For it is with your heart that you believe and are justified, and it is with your mouth that you profess your faith and are saved. As Scripture says, "Anyone who believes in him will never be put to shame." For there is no difference between Jew and Gentile—the same Lord is Lord of all and richly blesses all who call on him for "Everyone who calls on the name of the Lord will be saved."—Romans 10:9-13 NIV

DISCUSSION QUESTIONS

1. Where do you see a gap between what God has promised and what you currently experience, and how does that tension shape your faith right now?

2. When God's timing feels slow or his plan feels hidden, what habits or attitudes tend to surface in your life, and how might this chapter challenge those responses?

3. Israel struggled to believe God remembered them in their suffering. When have you felt forgotten by God, and what helped you hold on to truth instead of emotion?

4. This chapter highlights God working behind the scenes long before His people could see it. What is one area of your life where you need to trust that God is already at work even without visible evidence?

5. God's purpose continues even when His people feel stuck. What is one practical step you can take this week to align your actions with God's purpose rather than your discouragement?

END NOTES

[1] Luke 15:10, 20-24

[2] John 3:3-7; Galatians 4:4-7; Ephesians 1:5, 13-14; Romans 8:14-17, 23

[3] A person with two distinct personalities, one good, the other evil.

[4] John 10:2-4

[5] James 1:5

[6] Genesis 14:13-24

[7] Genesis 14:21

[8] Genesis 15:1, Abraham's name was Abram before God changed it to Abraham.

[9] Genesis 15:2-3

[10] Genesis 15:4

[11] Genesis 15:4-5 KJV

[12] Galatians 3:16

[13] 1 Corinthians 15:45-50, Romans 5:12-19

[14] Genesis 15:7

[15] Genesis 15:8

[16] John 8:56

[17] Hebrews 11:13

[18] Hebrews 11:10

[19] Matthew 20:25, Mark 10:41-42, Luke 22:25

[20] Genesis 47:5-6, Exodus 1:8-15 Jacob's family moved to Egypt in 1706 as a favored people. Pharaoh gave them the best land in Egypt and offered them positions as shepherds over his livestock. They prospered and multiplied until a regime change 111 years later. In 1595 their status changed from favored to an oppressed and afflicted people. Dates are taken from The Reese

Chronological Study Bible, by Edward Reese, Bethany House Publishers, Bloomington Minnesota 55438, Ebook edition, 2016.

[21] Genesis 22:1-19, Romans 4:12-13

[22] Genesis 28:10-15

[23] Genesis 28:20-22

[24] Genesis 31:1

[25] Genesis 31:3

[26] Genesis 31:13

[27] Genesis 33:4

[28] Genesis 35:1

[29] Genesis 35:2-3

[30] Joshua 24:23 NLT, is the only version to use destroy, other versions say remove. Israel would have understood Joshua's command through the lens of the law God gave to Moses, which told them to cut down, smash, burn idols and wipe out their names. Deuteronomy 12:3

[31] https://www.doctorwoodhead.com/nimrod-the-founder-of-the-occult-and-babylon/

[32] Josephus, Flavius Translated By William Whiston, The Works of Josephus Volume 2, Baker Book House Grand Rapids, Michigan, 1979, Antiquities of the Jews Book II Chapter XIII Pg. 79

[33] Ephesians 2:12 KJV

[34] Sir E. A. Wallis Budge, *Egyptian Ideas of the Future Life* (London: Keagan Paul, Trench, Truber & Co. LTD, 1908) 1

[35] Romans 1:20-23

[36] Matthew 15:9, Isaiah 29:13, Mark 7:7-8

[37] Romans 9:17, Exodus 9:16

[38] Thayers Greek Lexicon : 1) to arouse, raise up (from sleep) 2) to rouse up, stir up, incite. Exegeiro is used twice in the New Testament Romans 9:17 and 1 Corinthians 6:14. (bibletools.org, biblehub.com)

[39] Romans 9:18

[40] Ezekiel 33:11, 1 John 4:8, 1 Corinthians 13:1-8

[41] *"H2388 - ḥāzaq - Strong's Hebrew Lexicon (kjv)."* Blue Letter Bible. Web. 26 May, 2024. <https://www.blueletterbible.org/lexicon/h2388/kjv/wlc/0-1/>.

[42] *"H3513 - kāḇaḇ - Strong's Hebrew Lexicon (kjv)."* Blue Letter Bible. Web. 27 Jun, 2024. <https://www.blueletterbible.org/lexicon/h3513/kjv/wlc/2-1/#lexResults>.

[43] Romans 9:19-21

[44] Galatians 1:4

[45] Hebrews 11:13, 1 Peter 1:1, 2:11

[46] Hebrews 11:3

[47] Josephus, Flavius Translated By William Whiston, The Works of Josephus Volume 2, Baker Book House Grand Rapids, Michigan, 1979, Antiquities of the Jews Book II Chapter IX Pg. 153

[48] Acts 7:25 Amplified Bible

[49] Acts 7:27-28

[50] Exodus 2:11-14

[51] Acts 7:22

[52] Exodus 2:22

[53] John 8:56, Hebrews 11:24-27

[54] Moses saw a **bramble bush** which is any prickly shrub of the genus Rubus, which bears fruit like raspberries and blackberries.

[55] Exodus 3:5

[56] Exodus 3:7-10

[57] Exodus 3:12

[58] The Hebrew word translated as I AM means to exist.

[59] Exodus 4:1

[60] Exodus 4:10

[61] Acts 7:22

[62] Exodus 4:12

[63] Exodus 4:13

[64] אֱלֹהִים 'ĕlôhîym, el-o-heem'; plural of H433; Gods in the

ordinary sense; but specifically used (in the plural thus, especially with the article) of the supreme God

[65] Exodus 4:14-17

[66] Exodus 4:1-9, 4:29-31

[67] Ezekiel 20:5-8,

[68] Matthew 11:28-30

[69] Nahum M. Sarna, *Exploring Exodus* (Schocken Books, 1986), 55-56

[70] Exodus 3:18

[71] Exodus 5:1, 7:2

[72] Exodus 5:2

[73] What were a pharaoh's roles and responsibilities? - History Skills

[74] Matthew 11:29 NLT

[75] Exodus 5:3

[76] Exodus 5:5

[77] These two groups of people are call slave drivers and overseers in the NIV Bible, taskmaster and their officers in the KJV and NKJV, taskmasters and their foreman in the NASB95. Exodus 5:6 in the Amplified Bible says *"The very same day Pharaoh gave orders to the [Egyptian] taskmasters in charge of the people and their [Hebrew] officers..."*

[78] Exodus 5:8-9

[79] Numbers 23:19, 1 Samuel 15:29, Hebrews 6:18, Titus 1:2

[80] Isaiah 42:8, 48:11

[81] The KJV translates Strong's H7860 in the following manner: officers (23x), ruler (1x), overseer (1x).

[82] Exodus 5:14

[83] Exodus 5:15-16

[84] Exodus 5:17-18

[85] Exodus 5:21

[86] Exodus 5 :22-23

[87] 1 Peter 4:17-18, James 3:1

[88] Romans 2:9

[89] Romans 9:17

[90] Exodus 5:20

[91] Proverbs 13:24, 19:18, 23:13-14, Hebrews 12:6-11, Revelation 3:19

[92] Exodus 5:22-23, 6:1

[93] Exodus 6:2-3, Youngs Literal Translation. **H3068** יְהֹוָה yehôvâh From H1961; (the) *self Existent* or eternal; *God*, Jewish national name of God. For the evolution of God's name to God see Bible Projects video God's name has changed ?! (Learn its interesting Biblical History) https://youtu.be/eLrGM26pmM0?si=puXCDDWzAoj8hsud

[94] Myers, Teena, Faith's Mystery, (New Orleans LA: SCW Publishing 2023) p. 67-71

[95] The term *"God"* itself didn't appear until the Middle Ages. It arose when Christian scholars combined the consonants YHWH with the vowels of *"Adonai"* (meaning *"Lord"*), a substitution used in Jewish tradition to avoid pronouncing the sacred name aloud. So while *"God"* became popular in Christian circles, **ancient Israelites would have known their God as God**. The scholarly consensus is that God represents the older, original Hebrew divine name (YHWH), while Jehovah is a much later, Latinized hybrid that emerged in the Middle Ages. I am using God to distinguish the God of Abraham from the idols Egypt worshiped.

[96] Deuteronomy 29:29

[97] Exodus 6:7

[98] A Gentile is anyone who is not ethnically or religiously Jewish.

[99] Romans 5:18-21

[100] Hosea 4:6

[101] Exodus 7:8-9, https://israelmyglory.org/article/casting-down-serpents/

[102] Matthew 12:39

[103] Doxey, Denise, *"Priesthood",* in Redford, Donald B. (ed) (2001). *The Oxford Encyclopedia of Ancient Egypt.* Vol. III, pp. 69–70

[104] Josephus, Flavius Translated By William Whiston, The Works of Josephus Volume 2, Baker Book House Grand Rapids, Michigan, 1979, Antiquities of the Jews Book II Chapter XIII Pg. 165

[105] BBC - History - Ancient History in depth: Ancient Egyptian Magic

[106] On the symbolic role of serpents in Egyptian kingship and ritual power, see J. Baines, *"Symbolic Roles of Animals in Ancient Egypt,"* in Anthropozoologica 9 (1988): 99–108; R. K. Ritner, The Mechanics of Ancient Egyptian Magical Practice (Chicago: Oriental Institute, 1993), 105–112; and J. Assmann, The Mind of Egypt (Cambridge, MA: Harvard University Press, 2003), 72–75. These studies highlight the uraeus as a sign of divine sovereignty and the lector priest as a mediator of protective magic, providing essential context for interpreting the confrontation in Exod 7:8–13.

[107] Exodus 7:17

[108] Exodus 7:17-18

[109] Exodus 7:19

[110] Why the Nile River Was So Important to Ancient Egypt | HISTORY

[111] For discussions of the Nile's divine status and its role in Egyptian cosmology, see J. Assmann, *The Search for God in Ancient Egypt* (Ithaca: Cornell University Press, 2001), 34–41; K. A. Kitchen, *On the Reliability of the Old Testament* (Grand Rapids: Eerdmans, 2003), 249–252; and R. K. Ritner, *The Mechanics of Ancient Egyptian Magical Practice* (Chicago: Oriental Institute, 1993), 163–170.

[112] Exodus 7:24

[113] Isaiah 6:9, 44:18-20 / Matt 13:15 / Acts 28:24-28

[114] Exodus 8:1-2

[115] https://www.answerthebible.com/what-was-the-meaning-and-purpose-of-the-ten-plagues-of-egypt/

https://biblehub.com/topical/t/the_plague_of_frogs.htm

[116] What were a pharaoh's roles and responsibilities? - History Skills

[117] Exodus 8:8

[118] Matthew 12:37

[119] Romans 3:23

[120] 2 Peter 3:9

[121] Exodus 8:10

[122] 2 Corinthians 6:1-2

[123] Exodus 8:16 The Amplified Bible says *"[biting] gnats (lice)"*

[124] Luke 11:20

[125] For discussions of *heka*, priestly power, and divine agency in Egyptian religion, see J. Assmann, *The Search for God in Ancient Egypt* (Ithaca: Cornell University Press, 2001), 49–62; R. K. Ritner, *The Mechanics of Ancient Egyptian Magical Practice* (Chicago: Oriental Institute, 1993), 3–15; and S. Sauneron, *The Priests of Ancient Egypt* (Ithaca: Cornell University Press, 2000), 41–55.

[126] Genesis 43:32 & 46:34

[127] Matthew 13:14-15 AMP, Ezekiel 12:2 AMP

[128] 2 Corinthians 4:6-7; 2 Timothy 2:20-21

[129] Matthew 12:34-37

[130] Romans 5:20, KJV

[131] Matthew 7:24-27

[132] 2 Thessalonians 2:10

[133] The sandflies of Egypt suck blood and transmit disease. Their bites can cause a skin infection that produces lesions. The lesions heal slowly and may leave scars. The disease they transmit can also affect internal organs that can be fatal if left untreated.

[134] Exodus 8:20-23

[135] For Egyptian associations of flies with impurity, disorder, and divine withdrawal, see J. Assmann, *The*

Search for God in Ancient Egypt; S. Sauneron, The Priests of Ancient Egypt; and the UCLA Encyclopedia of Egyptology entries on ritual purity and *ma'at.*

[136] Exodus 8:25

[137] Exodus 8:28

[138] Exodus 8:29

[139] Romans 2:5

[140] Romans 2:1

[141] Exodus 9:1-5

[142] Mark, Joshua J.. ***"Ancient Egyptian Agriculture."*** *World History Encyclopedia.* World History Encyclopedia, 10 Jan 2017. Web. 12 Jul 2024.

[143] A boil is a specific type of lesion, but not all lesions are boils. Lesions is the umbrella term for any abnormal skin change, while boils are a distinct, pus-filled infection under that umbrella.

[144] Serge Sauneron, The Priests of Ancient Egypt, trans. David Lorton (Ithaca, NY: Cornell University Press, 2000), 35–38.

[145] Matthew 7:27, Deuteronomy 32:2, Ephesians 4:14, Hosea 8:7 Amplified Bible

[146] Reading the Plagues in their Ancient Egyptian Context - TheTorah.com

[147] Exodus 9:13-19

[148] Exodus 9:20-21

[149] Exodus 9:22

[150] **Storms as divine warfare in the ancient Near East**: Mark S. Smith, *The Origins of Biblical Monotheism* (Oxford: Oxford University Press, 2001), 47–72; Daniel Schwemer, *The Storm-Gods of the Ancient Near East* (Tübingen:Mohr Siebeck, 2008), 25–58. **Egyptian meteorology and theology**: Siegfried Morenz, *Egyptian Religion* (Ithaca: Cornell University Press, 1973), 113–118; Jan Assmann, *The Search for God in Ancient Egypt* (Ithaca: Cornell University Press, 2001), 55–63. **Hail and fire as signs of divine combat**: Patrick D. Miller, *"Fire in the Mythology*

of the Ancient Near East," Catholic Biblical Quarterly 27 (1965): 256–261; John Day, *Yahweh and the Gods and Goddesses of Canaan* (Sheffield: Sheffield Academic Press, 2000), 89–103. Within this cultural matrix, the Exodus narrative's unprecedented storm would have signaled not a natural anomaly but a direct theological challenge in which Israel's God asserts dominance over Egypt's gods and the natural domains they were believed to control.

[151] Exodus 9 :27

[152] Exodus 9:28

[153] Exodus 9:29-30

[154] Exodus 9:35

[155] Matthew 10:24, Luke 6:39-40, John 13:16

[156] 2 Peter 2:9 KJV

[157] Exodus 10:1

[158] Exodus 10:3-6

[159] Exodus 10:7

[160] Exodus 10:8

[161] I summarized Moses's response. He said, young and old. In the Hebrew Moses said na ar (nah-ar) Strongs #5288, which means, a boy from the age of infancy to adolescence; it can mean a servant or a girl. Yet in this verse the masculine narar is used not the feminine naarah meaning young girl. Moses said the narar, the male children and the zaqen (zawkane) Strongs #2205, which means old men. The feminine form of zaqen is zeqenah and refers to an old woman. Again in this verse the masculine zaqen is used not the feminine zeqenah. In all fairness Moses could have been referring to both sexes when he said young and old but the masculine form of both these words are used.

[162] Exodus 10:11

[163] Micah 6:4

[164] Women in Ancient Egypt - World History Encyclopedia/ Everything You Need to Know About Women in Ancient Egypt (pyramidsland.com)

[165] 1 Corinthians 12 :12-26

[166] See descriptions of the locust plague in Exodus 10:12–15 and commentary noting the unprecedented density and landscape-darkening effect of the swarm. https://www.sefaria.org/topics/plague-of-locusts?sort=Relevance&tab=notable-sources

[167] Lamentations 3:22-23

[168] Romans 5:20, KJV

[169] Romans 2:4-5

[170] Romans 4:18

[171] John 3:19

[172] Exodus 10:24

[173] Exodus 10:28

[174] Exodus 10:29, 11:4-8

[175] Exodus 11:8

[176] 2 Thessalonians 2:10

[177] 2 Thessalonians 2:10-12

[178] *"H7399 - rᵊḵûš - Strong's Hebrew Lexicon (niv)."* A general term for movable possession of all kinds. Blue Letter Bible. Web. 10 Jun, 2024. <https://www.blueletterbible.org/lexicon/h7399/niv/wlc/0-1/>.

[179] Exodus 3:21-22

[180] Deuteronomy 15:12-18

[181] Exodus 1:22

[182] A person with an unnaturally strong wish for power and control, or the belief that you are very much more important and powerful than you really are.

[183] 2 John 1:10-11

[184] Matthew 15:14

[185] Exodus 12:13

[186] Genesis 43:32, 46:34

[187] Exodus 12:31-32

[188] Exodus 12:33

[189] Proverbs 29:1 NKJ

[190] Galatians 6:7-8

[191] Galatians 6:7

[192] Exodus 14:5

[193] Exodus 14:6-9

[194] Exodus 13:20-22

[195] Exodus 14:11-12

[196] Exodus 14:19

[197] Deuteronomy 7:10

[198] Exodus 14:21-22

[199] Exodus 14:25

[200] Exodus 9:16, Romans 9:17

[201] Exodus 14:25

[202] Exodus 14:15-30

[203] Exodus 24:7

[204] Exodus 32:4 Amplified

[205] Numbers 14:34 King James Version

[206] Deuteronomy 8:4, 29:5 Clothes / Joshua 5:12 Manna / Exodus 13:22-21, 14:19-20, 40:36-38 Pillar Cloud & Fire

[207] Numbers 14:30-33

[208] Judges 2:10-13, 10:6, 10:13-14

[209] 1 Samuel 8:7

[210] 1 Kings 3:12, 4:30-31 / 2 Chronicles 1:12

[211] 1 Kings 12:26-30

[212] Ezekiel 8:6, The Living Bible

[213] Ezekiel 8:7-11 The Living Bible

[214] Ezekiel 8:12

[215] Acts 20:29-30 Paul used "savage wolves" as a metaphor to describe religious leaders who abuse God's people to enrich themselves. Jude 1:3-4, 10-13; Isaiah 32:6

[216] Acts 6:7

[217] Matthew 6:5-6, 16-17

[218] Matthew 17:1-5

[219] John 14:16-18, 16:13

[220] Ezekiel 36:26-27, John 14:15-18, Romans 8:11, 1 Corinthians 3:16, Galatians 4:6, 2 Timothy 1:14

[221] John 14:26, 16:13, 1 John 2:27

[222] Romans 12:2

[223] Matthew 15:16, 16:5-12, Mark 8:31-33, 9:9-10, 9:19 Luke 18:31-34, 22:36-51, 24:21 John 14:8-9

[224] 1 Corinthians 2:11-12

[225] Luke 24:45-49

[226] Romans 12:2

[227] Ephesians 4:14-15

[228] James 1:18

[229] Galatians 1 :12

[230] Galatians 4:19 AMP

[231] Ephesian 4:8 NKJ, Psalm 68:18 KJV, John 16:13

[232] James 1:17

[233] 2 Corinthians 10:3-6

[234] Philippians 2:12-13

[235] John 14:16-17, 26; 15:26, Luke 11:9-13

[236] Hebrews 4:1-11

[237] Numbers 14:22, Hebrews 3:11

[238] 1 Kings 3:10-12

[239] Hebrews 11:10

ABOUT THE AUTHOR

Teena Myers is the president of Southern Christian Writers, a fellowship of authors and poets dedicated to encouraging and equipping Christian creatives. She has served in Children's Church, worked in Christian television, taught Sunday School, and earned a Bachelor of Theology before discovering her true calling in writing.

Teena and her husband, Rory, produce *Voices of Inspiration*, which airs Mondays and Thursdays at 4 p.m. CST on Christian Mix 106.

She enjoys spending time with her children and grandchildren, training for triathlons, and savoring quiet evenings in the empty nest she shares with her husband.

OTHER BOOKS

Faith's Mystery: Understanding Faith That Pleases God

CONTACT

teena@teenamyers.com

scwguild.com

teenamyers.com

Facebook.com/scwguild

linkedin.com/in/teena-myers

www.ingramcontent.com/pod-product-compliance
Lightning Source LLC
LaVergne TN
LVHW020644100826
845148LV00012B/2327